THe 57 BUS

DASHKA SLATER

THe
57
BUS
DASHKA SLATER

First published in Great Britain in 2018 by Wren & Rook
Published by arrangement with Rights People, London

First published in 2017 by Farrar Straus Giroux Books for Young Readers
An imprint of Macmillan Publishing Group, LLC
175 Fifth Avenue, New York, NY 10010

ISBN: 978 1 5263 6123 3
10 9 8 7 6 5 4 3

Wren & Rook
An imprint of Hachette Children's Group
Part of Hodder & Stoughton
Carmelite House
50 Victoria Embankment
London EC4Y 0DZ
An Hachette UK Company
www.hachette.co.uk
www.hachettechildrens.co.uk

Printed in England

Publishing Director: Debbie Foy
Senior Editor: Elizabeth Brent
Designed by Laura Hambleton and Anne Diebel
Cover design by Thy Bui

For Cliff

CONTENTS

PART 2: Richard   71

PART 3: The Fire   117

This is a true story. All the people in this book are real, although in some cases pseudonyms or initials were used. Young people are identified by first name only.

The details of the story were pieced together from a variety of sources, including interviews, documents, letters, videos, diaries, social media posts, and public records. Quotes from these sources are verbatim except in a few cases where I removed last names, replacing them with long dashes. Information from firsthand accounts was corroborated with official records wherever possible, unless those records were sealed or are not available to the public. In those cases, I relied on the memory of witnesses and participants.

The pronouns and names used for gender-nonconforming people were approved by the people in question.

By four-thirty in the afternoon, the first mad rush of after-school passengers has come and gone. What's left are stragglers and stay-laters, swiping their bus passes as they climb on to the 57 bus and take seats among the coming-home workers, the shoppers and errand-doers, the other students from high schools and middle schools around the city. The bus is loud but not as loud as sometimes. A few clusters of kids are shouting and laughing and an older woman at the front keeps talking to the driver.

Dark is coming on. Daylight saving time ended yesterday, and now evening rushes into the place where afternoon used to be. Everything is duskier, sleepier, wintrier now. Passengers look at their phones or stare through the scratched and grimy windows at the waning light.

Sasha sits near the back. For much of the journey, the teenager

17

has been reading a paperback copy of *Anna Karenina* for a class in Russian literature. Today, like most days, Sasha wears a T-shirt, a black fleece jacket, a gray flat cap and a gauzy white skirt. In the final, senior, year at a small private high school, the teenager identifies as agender – neither male nor female. As the bus lumbers through town, Sasha puts down the book and drifts into sleep, skirt draped over the edge of the seat.

A few feet away, three teenage boys are laughing and joking. One of them, Richard, wears a black hoodie and an orange-billed New York Knicks hat. A sixteen-year-old in his penultimate, junior, year at Oakland High School, he's got hazel eyes and a slow, sweet grin. He stands with his back to Sasha, gripping a pole for balance.

Sasha sleeps as Richard and his companions goof around, play fighting. Sleeps as Richard's cousin Lloyd bounds up and down the aisle flirting with a girl at the front. Sleeps as Richard surreptitiously flicks a lighter and touches it to the hem of that gauzy white skirt.

Wait.

In a moment, Sasha will wake up inside a ball of flame and begin to scream.

In a moment, everything will be set in motion.

Taken by ambulance to a San Francisco burn unit, Sasha will spend the next three and a half weeks undergoing multiple operations to treat second- and third-degree burns running from calf to thigh.

Arrested at school the following day, Richard will be charged with two felonies, each with a hate-crime clause that will add time to his sentence if he is convicted. Citing the severity of the crime, the district attorney (the chief prosecutor of the area) will charge him as an adult, stripping him of the protections normally given to juvenile offenders. Before the week is out, he will be facing the possibility of life imprisonment.

But none of that has happened yet. For now, both teenagers are just taking the bus home from school.

Surely it's not too late to stop things from going wrong. There must be some way to wake Sasha. Divert Richard. Get the driver to stop the bus.

There must be something you can do.

Oakland, California, is a city of more than 400,000 people, but it can still feel like a small town. Not small geographically, of course. The city sprawls across seventy-eight square miles, stretching from the shallow, salty estuary at the edge of San Francisco Bay to the undulating green-and-gold hills where bobcats and coyotes roam. What makes it feel small is the web of connections, the way people's stories tangle together. Our lives make footprints, tracks in the snows of time. People know each other's parents or siblings, their aunties and cousins. They go to school together, or worship together. They play sport on the same team, or work in the same building. The tracks cross. The stories overlap.

Oakland is considered one of the most diverse cities in the US. It's Asian and Latino, black and white, African, Arab, Indian, Iranian, Native American and Pacific Islander. No one group is a majority. It has more lesbian couples per capita than any city in America, and one of the largest proportions of gay- and lesbian-headed households. It's a city that prides itself on its open-mindedness, its lack of pretension and its homegrown slang. (Oaklanders say *hella* when they mean *very* – and *hecka* when they want to be polite about it.)

But for all its laid-back inclusiveness, Oakland is also a city of stark contrasts. In 2013, the year Sasha was burned, Oakland ranked seventh among American cities in income inequality – just below New York. Its per capita rate of violent crime made it the second most dangerous city in America, but its citizens still paid some of the highest rents in the country.

Gravity works backwards here – the money flows uphill. The wealthier neighbourhoods in the hills boast good schools, low crime and views of the bay. Thanks to the San Francisco Bay Area's high-tech boom, long-vacant historic buildings downtown are filling with start-ups, boutiques peddling handmade jeans and nightspots serving seven-ingredient cocktails. But little of this good fortune spilled over into the flatlands of East Oakland, where Richard lived. This is where the bulk of the city's murders happen – two-thirds of them in 2013. The schools are shabbier here; the test scores are lower. There's more rubbish on the streets, more roaming dogs, more liquor stores, fewer grocery stores. The central reservations are ragged with weeds.

The 57 bus travels through both kinds of neighbourhood, traversing an eleven-mile path from one end of the city to the other. It begins at the northwest corner of Oakland and lumbers diagonally through the city, crossing the middle-class foothills where Sasha lived and where Richard went to school, and then chugging along MacArthur Boulevard for 120 blocks. The route terminates at the city's southeast border, close to Richard's house. Each afternoon, the two teenagers' journeys overlapped for a mere eight minutes. If it hadn't been for the 57 bus, their paths might never have crossed at all.

PART 1
SASHA

TUMBLING

(Adapted from Sasha's Tumblr page)

Favorite vegetable: bok choy
Favorite animals: cat and cuttlefish
Favorite type of movie: dream sequences

Three best qualities?
Navigation
      My friends seem to like me
          Purple

Of course I like hats
anyone who doesn't is wrong

I like compliments
I dislike compliments
I like my hair
          I give good hugs

I'm good at finding potential puns.

If the whole world was listening, I might just
                rant about a bunch of things like gender
        wealth inequality
                why school is important

I like parties
I dislike parties

I don't really keep track of disappointments.

Ideal vacation spot: prob'ly a city with a nice subway

Thinking of things to get me? Try this:
A brass airship
        A transit map shower curtain
                A medieval cloak
                        A corset with silver buttons
        A chiseled chunk of gallium that melts in your palm
A dress swirled with the image of a nebula
        A Victorian house on wheels
                Tights painted like a mermaid tail

Even as a toddler, Sasha was interested in language. Not in learning Italian or Swahili or Mandarin, but in language itself, its shape and structure, the Lego blocks of sounds that snap together to make words and sentences. Most toddlers are interested in the fact that the animal with two pointy ears and a long tail is called a *cat*. Sasha was interested in the fact that adding an *s* at the end of the word *cat* made it plural. 'Look,' Sasha would say. 'Two cat ... sssss.'

Before turning three, Sasha was matching sounds with letters – sometimes in unusual ways. '*B* is for *baby*!' Sasha would exclaim. '*Y* is for *wire*! *Ten* is for *tent*!'

At four, Sasha was reading independently, but had also begun contemplating the shapes of letters. '*K* is one rectangle and two parallelograms,' Sasha announced at the breakfast table one day. '*M* is two parallelograms and two rectangles.'

Two years later, Sasha began creating a new language. It was called Astrolinguish and it was the language of Sasha's home planet, Astrolingua. Written Astrolinguish was awash in diacritical marks, with lots of umlauts, accents and tildes. The spoken language luxuriated in rolled *r*'s and *l*'s.

As a senior in high school, Sasha was still inventing languages, hanging out online with other 'conlangers' – people who construct languages of their own. By now Sasha was working up a new language. This one never had a name, but it was spoken by the members of an imaginary agricultural society something like that of ancient Mesopotamia.

All languages embody the obsessions of the people who speak them, and so Sasha's language was meant to reflect the interests of a people whose world was dominated by growing seasons, grains and harvests. Instead of pronouns that distinguished between male and female, Sasha's language had pronouns that distinguished between animate and inanimate objects. The word for *sun* was *jejz*, which was also the word for *day*. The difference was that *sun* was considered animate, a being, and *day* was considered inanimate, a thing.

Our language, English, works differently. We care a lot about gender, and English reflects that in its pronouns – *she* or *he*, *her* or *him*, *hers* or *his*. You might think this is just how languages work in the real world, but there are many languages on earth that are basically gender neutral, using the same word for *he*, *she* and *it*, or not using pronouns at all. You've probably heard of some of them. They include: Armenian, Comanche, Finnish, Hungarian, Hindi, Indonesian, Quechua, Thai, Tagalog, Turkish, Vietnamese and Yoruba.

English, on the other hand, poses a challenge for people like Sasha who don't see themselves as fitting into neat either/or categories like male or female. Sasha, like many gender-nonconforming people, wants to be referred to with the pronoun *they*. It might feel awkward at first, but you'll get used to it.

For their sixteenth birthday, Sasha asked for an accordion, a manual typewriter, a Soviet flag and a new Rubik's Cube. They didn't know how to play the accordion, but they might have learned if they had received one, which they didn't. They didn't get the flag either, although Sasha and their friend Michael made a cardboard hammer and sickle not long afterward and hung it on Sasha's bedroom wall. At the time, they were obsessed with everything to do with Russia and communism. Their friend Carrie, who took the bus with Sasha that year, remembers Sasha going on and on about it during the bus ride home from school.

'Sasha, once you get to know them, is very outspoken about things,' she explains.

That's once you get to know them. When you first meet Sasha, they're quiet and shy. They have chin-length, wavy brown hair, a pale, round face, and thick, dark eyebrows. When they smile, their eyes crinkle into slits. They wear glasses, round owlish ones, and they don't always look at you straight on. As a child they were diagnosed with Asperger's, a form of autism, which can make them awkward socially. But it also makes them passionate about their interests, and the passion eventually trumps the shyness.

What was Sasha passionate about when they were in the senior year of high school? 'Buses, cartoons and the colour purple,' says Healy, one of Sasha's closest friends. To that you could add communism, games, the web comic *Homestuck*, and live-action role-playing or larping. Also the ska-pop-punk band Sarchasm, which was formed by some kids at Maybeck High School and had once proclaimed Sasha their biggest fan. And veganism, although Sasha disliked the way other vegans on the Internet made such a huge deal about it.

Sasha's best friend was Michael, a tall, gangly kid with sandy-blonde hair and thick glasses who always wore a gray beanie and a green army jacket. Michael and Sasha had been pretty much inseparable since the first, freshman, year of high school, when they met while playing the board game Diplomacy. Over time, they formed the nucleus of a tight circle of friends: Sasha, Healy, Michael, Michael's girlfriend Teah, and another friend named Ian. Ian, blonde, bearded, with a habit of tucking his chin and looking up at you from under his eyebrows, was the one who never stopped talking. Red-haired Healy was the unquellable fountain of excitement who stole people's hats and wore her emotions on her sleeve. Cherub-faced Teah loved costumes and dancing – she and Michael were so close that their friends referred to them as a single person named Tichael. When the two got too cuddly, Sasha would get between them and shout, 'Leave room for Jesus!' at the top of their lungs, like the chaperone at a Christian prom.

Sasha was the brilliant one, the one who blazed through

calculus, linguistics, physics and computer programming with a kind of effortlessness. Not that any of them were slouches when it came to academics. Kids who weren't into school were unlikely to choose Maybeck, a private high school with roughly a hundred kids that rented space on two floors of a Presbyterian church in Berkeley, north of Oakland. In the tiny classrooms, students gathered around conference tables and critiqued the concept of America as a shining city on a hill, or compared the writings of Charles Darwin and Ursula K. Le Guin.

Teachers liked to claim that Maybeck didn't have cliques like other high schools, and it was true that the place was a refuge for kids like Healy who had been bullied in middle school. People were nice to each other at Maybeck, accepting. But the school still had social groupings, just like any other high school – arty kids, stoners, bros.

'We were the nerdy kids,' Ian says. 'The funny, sort of crazy, nerdy people who played video games and watched anime and read manga.'

All of them were fascinated by games – board games, video games, card games, role-playing games, trading-card games. At lunch and after school they often gathered at a wooden table in the hallway that people called the hex table, even though, as Ian pointed out, it was an octagon, not a hexagon. There they played cards, particularly a game Michael and Sasha had learned from a couple of seniors when they were freshmen. It was officially called 1001 Blank White Cards, although they mostly just called it Index Cards.

'It's a game played with index cards,' Sasha explains. 'Not all of which are white and at this point very few of which are blank.' The deck grew over time, with people pilfering index cards from classrooms whenever they wanted to expand it. If you drew a blank card from the deck, that meant you could fill it in, assigning it a point value and an effect, the more random the better. Over time, the deck filled up with in-jokes.

There was a card featuring a drawing of *The Sun Also Rises* by Ernest Hemingway that resulted in the player losing two turns *as you read the book and are bored to death*. There was a card that required you to talk in a Russian accent, a card that required you to lisp, and a card that required you to lisp while talking in a Russian accent. There were cards that required you to play an air guitar solo, speak like an English-dubbed anime character, eat leaves like a giraffe, engage in staring contests, and end every sentence with the word *dawg*. There was a card called Tower of Hats that required you to take everyone else's hats and wear them in a stack. There was a card that said *Game over, Ian wins!* that had been created as a birthday present for Ian. Sasha created a card called *A Complete History of the Soviet Union as Told by a Humble Worker, Arranged to the Melody of Tetris*, which was the name of a six-and-a-half-minute song by an obscure British comedy band called Pig with the Face of a Boy. Michael and Sasha were both obsessed with the song and sang it at every opportunity. 'The effect of the card is that you have to sing the song or lose a turn,' Sasha explains.

Aside from Ian's birthday card, there was no way to win the game, and no real goal. They just played until people had to go home. By graduation, the stack of index cards was about two feet

33

high and had to be carried in a special bag. But at the beginning, most of those 1001 white cards were blank. Back then, Sasha was called Luke and they were referred to as *he*.

In middle school, Sasha was brainy, shy and introverted, the kind of kid who is easy to overlook. Sasha's father, Karl, refers to that quality as Sasha's 'invisibility cloak'. 'They blend into the background,' he explains. 'They've always been that sort of kid, that nobody even knows they're there.'

Sasha didn't seem to need other people much; in fact, they often said that the world would be better off without humans in it at all. The world inside their head was fascinating enough. They thought about numbers a lot, and shapes and the size of the universe. They drew imaginary subway maps and worked out maths problems on a whiteboard the family kept in the breakfast nook. They were interested in space and Lego and trains and the ancient Greeks and they noticed things most people didn't, like the subtle shades within the green of a leaf, or the geometric shapes within a sculpture. They loved cats and had a habit of meowing. Sasha couldn't say whether any of this was because they had Asperger's, because, of course, they'd never *not* had Asperger's. The only mind they'd ever been inside was their own.

When they were 11, Sasha started attending a tiny Montessori school with about twenty-five kids in each year. They were in a mixed-age class of 9–12 year olds, and there was just one other new kid that year, an apple-cheeked 10 year old named Samantha. She looked right past Sasha's invisibility cloak and saw a kindred spirit.

Samantha was a head taller than Sasha, with tousled blond hair, ivory skin that flushed easily and wire-rimmed glasses. Her family moved around a lot, and at ten she'd already lived in five states and attended six different schools. But she had never had a best friend. She was used to being an outcast, to feeling both smarter than other kids, and stupider. Her dad was a nanotechnologist whose laboratory was in their basement. He'd been giving her what he called 'Dad Homework' for her whole life and she'd always gotten pleasure from demonstrating her intelligence. Yet she could never seem to learn the rules that other kids played by, the rules that defined how you were supposed to talk and how you were supposed to look and what you were supposed to be interested in. Rules that defined how smart was *too* smart.

Samantha noticed that Sasha wrote their name on homework assignments in Greek letters. She noticed that Sasha loved maths and costumes and imaginary worlds. She noticed how passionate Sasha was about everything – their conviction that the ancient Greeks were better than the ancient Romans, that base twelve counting was better than base ten, that cats were better than dogs. She noticed Sasha's long eyelashes, and their curly, shoulder-length brown hair.

'Samantha has a crush on me,' Sasha told Karl, with a kind of anthropological interest. And it was true; she did. It didn't take long for the two of them to become inseparable. Sasha adopted Samantha's way of talking – pronouncing 'Fail!' when something was lame and 'Lol!' when something was funny. They played Dungeons & Dragons and then left the twelve-sided die on the floor and invented magical battles of their own. They each adopted a tiny, invisible baby dragon – Sasha's was named Cinnamon, Samantha's was Pendragon. They invented stupid TV shows, unleashing a cavalcade of ever-increasing banality as they tried to out-stupid each other. They were so close that Samantha felt like Sasha was inside her head, thinking her thoughts before she'd even thought them herself.

That closeness, of course, drew the attention of their classmates. As far as anyone could tell, Samantha was a girl and Sasha was a boy. The teasing was merciless. Everyone wanted to know if they were boyfriend and girlfriend, if they were K-I-S-S-I-N-G. (They weren't.) It drove Samantha crazy. She once grabbed a classmate by the arm, yelling, *'Stop making fun of us!'*. Her fingers hit a pressure point and the girl screamed in pain. Samantha felt terrible about it. But still. Why couldn't everyone just leave them alone?

It was part of that disorienting feeling she'd had for years, that feeling that everyone except her had been issued a handbook. Samantha knew it was important to be pretty and cute, but she had no idea how to be those things, or even why she was supposed to want to be. Her body was growing curvier. Breasts burst from her chest like twin cannonballs, but they didn't feel sexy and good, they just felt heavy. She hid them under baggy T-shirts and sweatshirts and watched the other girls come to school in tiny skirts and spaghetti straps, wondering why everything was so much harder for her than it was for them.

'Tell me how to be popular,' she begged one of the spaghetti-strap girls. The girl's expression – her lowered eyes, the way she glanced around, seeking escape – told Samantha what a mistake the question had been. *If you have to ask, it's out of reach.*

Something was wrong with her, really wrong. She was angry. She was sad. She was afraid. She wanted to die. In sixth grade, she said so in class. Her teacher told her parents, who took her to a therapist.

One day Samantha told the therapist about a video she'd seen on YouTube. Two young women stood back-to-back performing a slam poem called 'Hir,' rotating to face the mic as they gave voice to a girl named Melissa and the boy inside her named James.

> *Sometimes she wishes she could rip the skin*
>   *off her back,*
> *Every moment of every day she feels*
>   *trapped in the flesh of a stranger.*

Watching it, Samantha felt something chime inside her – a bell vibrating in resonance. Before puberty, her physical body didn't seem to have that much to do with who she was. People used to mistake her for a boy, but she had felt proud to be a girl. But now being a girl was like being stuffed into a heavy, constricting costume. She could barely breathe in it. The rules of the universe were fixed: You look a certain way and so you have to act a certain way and people are going to treat you a certain way. There was no way to alter it.

'I think I might be ... transgender?' she whispered to her therapist the next week.

'I don't think you know what *transgender* means,' her therapist replied.

The bell that had been chiming inside her fell silent. She's the expert, Samantha thought.

It would be another year before she told anyone else.

Sasha and Samantha were playing *Gran Turismo 2* in Sasha's basement. Samantha was thirteen; Sasha was fourteen.

Samantha took a breath. 'I have something really important to tell you.'

Sasha's eyes were on the screen where their two cars were racing. 'What?'

'I'm transgender.'

She told Sasha about the way she'd been feeling and about the response she'd had from her therapist the year before.

'You're the only one who knows what you feel,' Sasha said. 'If that's the word for what you feel, then stick with that. Now, what's the important thing you had to tell me?'

Five years later, a handsome, apple-cheeked young man named Andrew would look back at that conversation as one of the most validating moments of his life. 'It wasn't that I was expecting Sasha to react poorly, because I know Sasha, and Sasha is easily one of the smartest people I've ever met and also one of the kindest,' he recalled. 'But taking a risk like that and having everything be OK afterward felt so good.'

Back then though, Andrew rarely spoke about gender with Sasha after that one conversation. He wouldn't tell his parents he was trans for another year. For a while he convinced himself that being a girl would be OK, that being trans was just too hard a life. A year later, Andrew was Sasha's date to the Maybeck prom. He wore a bottle-green dress and bloodred lipstick, and his hair was dyed coppery orange. But it was still just a costume – the dress, the lipstick, the hair, the body. By the time he started high school in the autumn, Andrew had already begun his gender transition.

Sasha and Andrew were hanging out in Sasha's bedroom. It was the winter of 2012. Sasha was in their second year at Maybeck High School, and Andrew was a freshman at a public high school nearby. Sasha was at the computer, showing Andrew the ins and outs of the board game Diplomacy.

'Andrew?' Sasha said. 'I don't know if this is rude or not, but I was wondering how you realised you were a guy?'

'I just knew I wasn't a girl,' Andrew explained. 'I just knew that was not who I was at all.'

Andrew had recently been hospitalised after contemplating suicide. Even though he'd started high school as a boy, his trans status was a topic of constant rumour and gossip. People at school kept coming up and saying awkward and nonsensical things like 'I heard you got a sex transplant?' And then his mother had a psychotic episode and his grandfather died and it was just too much all at once. Now, as Sasha explained that they also were questioning their gender, Andrew felt a rush of relief, similar to the one he'd felt when he came out to Sasha.

'The fact that someone like Sasha, who I respected so much, was also going through this – it was another thank-God moment,' Andrew remembered later. 'Like, I'm not such a weird person.'

Not everyone had that reaction though. For most people, the question was kind of mysterious. 'I just know,' Sasha's father, Karl, said when Sasha asked how he knew he was a man. 'It's who I am.'

That seemed to be true for most people. They just *knew*. Whether or not the appearance of their body matched the gender in their mind, there was some core understanding: my identity is *this*.

But Sasha didn't feel that. Didn't feel strongly *This is what I am*. Didn't feel strongly *This is what I'm not*. Other people seemed to have a file in their brain marked *Gender*. Sasha ransacked their own brain looking for the file, but it didn't seem to be there.

So what did that mean? The idea of not having a gender wasn't frightening to Sasha, but it wasn't a relief either. Maybe this is just a phase, Sasha thought. Maybe I'm just overthinking things.

But maybe not. Maybe the question was its own kind of answer. Maybe the place in between was a real place.

'For me at least, *genderqueer* includes an aspect of questioning,' Sasha explains. 'The fact that I was questioning my gender meant that I was genderqueer.'

Still, Sasha kept probing. On Facebook, they posted a status update asking, *What is your preferred pronoun?*

'Your Highness,' Karl quipped. But afterwards, he asked Sasha what the question meant.

Sasha explained that there were other choices besides *he* and s*he*, choices like *it*, or *they*, or more recently invented gender-neutral pronouns like *ne*, *ve* and *ze* or *xe*. Listening, it became clear to Karl that this was a topic Sasha had been thinking about a lot.

Not long afterwards, Sasha was talking with their parents about someone they'd met online who identified as genderqueer.

'Are *you* genderqueer?' asked Debbie, Sasha's mother.

'Yeah,' Sasha said.

That was the extent of the conversation. But that night, Sasha posted on Google+: *Just came out as genderqueer to my parents. Basically, I don't identify as masculine or feminine.*

Reading the post, and the congratulatory comments that followed it, Debbie and Karl were left scratching their heads. Apparently something big had just happened, but they weren't entirely sure what it was.

What did *genderqueer* even mean?

Debbie and Karl had always had a good relationship with Sasha. As a family, they joked around a lot, but they also talked seriously about the stuff that mattered. And clearly this gender stuff mattered to Sasha. Only it was kind of hard to figure out why. Was this about sex? About love? About changing your body?

'I'm trying to get my head around it,' Debbie said two years after that first conversation. 'I understand coming out as gay or even trans, but this is harder for me to understand.'

She and Karl were sitting side by side on the claret-coloured sofa in their living room, framed by the bay window behind them. They live in a snug green bungalow in Oakland's Glenview district, about a mile from Oakland High School. Debbie, who works as a bookkeeper at a private school, has a mobile, expressive face framed by blonde chin-length hair. Her gestures are broad and comic. Karl is shyer and quieter. A former college radio DJ turned kindergarten teacher, he has a gentle, thoughtful manner punctuated by a dry wit. He wears his silvering hair short on the sides and has a rainbow friendship bracelet tied around one wrist.

Debbie's mind kept going to the sex part. Who did Sasha want to sleep with? After Sasha announced they were genderqueer, she asked for clarification. 'Who are you attracted to? Do you have sexual feelings for men?'

But that wasn't the issue for Sasha. They weren't all that interested in having sex with anyone, actually. And anyway, terms like *homosexual* or *heterosexual* made no sense if you didn't identify as one gender or another.

Most of us see gender, sexuality and romance as one big interconnected tangle of feelings – this is who I am, this is who I'm attracted to, this is who I love. But as Sasha began exploring the topic online, they found that some people had developed language for combing the tangle into individual strands.

In these online conversations, the word *sex* referred purely to biology – the chromosomes, organs and anatomy that define male and female from the outside. *Gender* was the word for what people felt about themselves, how they felt *inside*. *Sexuality* was the category for who you were physically attracted to. *Romantic* was the category for who you felt romantic attraction to. And there was a whole array of distinctions within each category as well. It was like a gigantic menu, with columns and columns of choices.

GENDER, SEX, SEXUALITY, ROMANCE: SOME TERMS

Because language is evolving rapidly, and because different people have different preferences, always adopt the language individuals use about themselves, even if it differs from what's here.

TERMS FOR GENDER AND SEX

agender/neutrois – Doesn't identify as any gender.

androgynous – Identifies as a third gender that blends male and female characteristics.

bigender/gender fluid – Sometimes identifies as male and sometimes as female.

cis/cisgender – The opposite of transgender; gender matches their birth sex.

gender questioning – Is unsure about where they belong on the gender spectrum.

genderqueer/nonbinary – Gender identity doesn't fit neatly into male/female categories.

intersex – Born with sexual anatomy, organs, or chromosomes that don't seem to fit the typical definitions of female or male. Replaces the outdated and offensive term *hermaphrodite.*

trans/transgender – Feels their gender is different from their birth sex, whether or not they have physically changed their body or outward presentation. A transgender man is someone who currently identifies as male. A transgender woman is someone who currently identifies as female.

TERMS FOR SEXUALITY

asexual – Not physically attracted to anyone.

bisexual – Physically attracted to both men and women.

cupiosexual – Doesn't feel sexual attraction, but is still interested in sex.

graysexual – Mostly doesn't feel sexual attraction but does occasionally.

heterosexual – Physically attracted to people of the opposite gender.

homosexual – Physically attracted to people of the same gender.

pansexual – Physically attracted to people across the gender spectrum.

TERMS FOR ROMANTIC INCLINATION

aromantic – Not romantically attracted to anyone.

biromantic – Romantically attracted to both men and women.

cupioromantic – Doesn't feel romantic attraction, but is still interested in romance.

heteroromantic – Romantically attracted to people of the opposite gender.

homoromantic – Romantically attracted to people of the same gender.

panromantic – Romantically attracted to people across the gender spectrum.

quoiromantic – Doesn't understand the difference between romantic and platonic love.

SASHA'S TERMS

In the end, these were the terms Sasha felt described them best:

Agender.

Gray-cupiosexual.

Quoiromantic.

Also: Vegan.

BECOMING SASHA

Discovering the existence of genderqueer identity felt like discovering a secret room. All this time there had been just two rooms: male and female. Now it turned out there was another room – one that could be furnished however you wanted. The more time Sasha spent in this room, the more comfortable it felt. But the person who lived in this new room still had a boy's name – Luke. As they moved through the second year of Maybeck, that name clearly no longer fit.

One afternoon, when Andrew was hanging out at Sasha's house, the two of them began looking at unisex names on Wikipedia.

Jamie. Shannon. Taylor.

Fran. Jackie. Kris. Bobby.

Kai. Parker. Quinn.

Sasha.

Sasha was the Russian nickname for both Alexandra and Alexander, which was Sasha's middle name. And Sasha was crazy about all things Russian. The name was perfect.

Gradually, Sasha asked their parents and close friends to call them Sasha instead of Luke. That spring, Sasha wrote a piece for the Maybeck school zine, *The Pineapple*, about their exploration of gender. They used their new name as the byline.

Most people at school had no idea who this Sasha person was. But as students and staff made the connection between Sasha and the Person Formerly Known as Luke, they absorbed the information without much comment. 'It wasn't really drama,' Michael recalls. 'It was just a change.'

Ian has two mums, so he was pretty comfortable with LGBTQ stuff. He remembers his thought process going like this: *OK, not male. OK, not female. So, neither? OK.* 'That was the process and it took about ten seconds,' he says. 'Then it was over.'

'I just rolled with the fact that Sasha was agender,' Teah says. 'I think it was my first experience with it, but I was raised by hippies.' At another school, a student who stepped outside the usual gender categories might have been the topic of gossip or debate or at least a few raised eyebrows. But Maybeck's small student body already included one student who was agender and two who were transgender.

'Multiple people would come out and you'd be like, OK, they're this and they use this name and this pronoun now,' says Sasha's friend Carrie. 'I mean, like, not everyone was good at it, but the people who were friends with trans people were.'

The friends who made the effort to get it right gave Sasha the confidence to correct the acquaintances who got it wrong. And more and more, the pronoun *he* felt wrong.

'I don't want for people to think of me as a *he*, and when they say *he*, not only does it reinforce in their brains that I *am* a he, it also reinforces it in the brains of the people who are listening,' Sasha explains. 'It doesn't really directly affect me, at least to hear it – it's more like, *Huh, that's not right.* And when people use the right pronouns, when they use *they* or another gender-neutral pronoun, it feels validating.'

A card called Luke … Sasha … Person was added to the index card deck. *If someone calls Sasha by the wrong name*, the card instructed, *the offender must discard a card from his/her hand.*

BATHROOMS

Sometimes, Debbie felt as she stood at the petrol station, the whole nonbinary thing was a pain in the ass. It was Thanksgiving 2012, Sasha's penultimate year of high school. Debbie, Karl and Sasha were driving to southern California to spend the holiday with Debbie's sister. A couple of hours in, Sasha had requested a bathroom stop, which was why they were now parked at a petrol station off the highway. But Sasha had surveyed the two options – Men and Women – and walked back to the car.

'There's no bathroom for me,' they said, climbing into the backseat.

Debbie was furious. Was this really how Sasha was going to go through life – with their bladder full to bursting?

'It's not healthy,' she fumed. 'There's not always going to be a bathroom available for you. You have to be more flexible.'

But Sasha refused to budge. They held it in for the rest of the six-hour drive.

It was tough sometimes, watching Sasha navigate a world that didn't even have a category for them. Occasionally, Debbie wished Sasha would ease up a little – resist correcting well-meaning relatives who said *he* instead of *they*, for example. But there was something admirable about it, too, Karl pointed out. Knowing how shy Sasha was, he admired Sasha's newfound willingness to speak up, to stand out, to be seen.

'I wonder, if Sasha hadn't been in a school where alternatives to the norm were part of the culture and accepted, if they would have been struggling more to figure out where they fit in the scheme of things,' he said. 'It feels like making this discovery has really helped Sasha become themself.'

BATHROOMS REVISITED

Over the course of the next year, Sasha found a way to deal with the problem of bathrooms.

At Maybeck, they used the staff bathroom.

Out in the world, they used whatever bathroom had the shortest line, whatever bathroom was closer, or whatever bathroom was least conspicuous.

If they had to use the bathroom multiple times in one place, they alternated. Nobody seemed to care which bathroom they used. Or if they did, Sasha didn't notice.

SKIRTS

Sasha wore a skirt for the first time during their second year of high school, on Maybeck's annual cross-dressing day. This was before they started thinking about gender, when dressing up as a girl was just a gag that the whole school was taking part in, everyone, regardless of orientation, clothed in exaggerated masculine or feminine costumes. Sasha borrowed a skirt from their friend Carrie, who lived in Sasha's neighbourhood. What struck them then was how comfortable it was to wear one.

In January 2013, when Sasha was in their penultimate year at Maybeck, they turned to Carrie again.

'I don't have any feminine clothes,' they complained. Sasha had been identifying as agender for almost a year by now, but they still dressed the same as they always had – like a boy.

'I have *lots* of feminine clothes,' Carrie replied. 'Too many!'

She brought a bag full of hand-me-downs to school – mostly skirts she'd worn when she was younger. Sasha sifted through them, and after trying on a few skirts in the bathroom, chose three to take home. Aside from during one school trip to China, they never wore trousers again.

Previously Sasha's style had tended toward steampunk – top hat and tweeds, vests, bow ties, even a pocket watch and a pair of fighter-pilot goggles. Sasha liked the sartorial gender mash-up that came from adding a skirt to this ensemble – masculine above, feminine below. But there were plenty of days when they didn't bother getting fancy, pairing one of Carrie's old skirts with a T-shirt and kneesocks.

The outfits weren't flamboyant, but they made Debbie nervous. She knew Sasha would be fine at school – if anything, the skirts gave them a little extra cachet at Maybeck, where unconventionality was an asset. It was the bus that worried her. Wearing skirts meant that Sasha was shedding that cloak of invisibility. Now they weren't just visible, but conspicuous. And outside of the cocoon of Maybeck High School, being conspicuous wasn't always a good idea.

Transgender people are the victims of an astonishing amount of violence. One out of every four trans people has experienced a bias-driven assault, and the numbers are higher for trans women, trans people of colour, and people who identify as neither male nor female. Of the 860 nonbinary people who responded to the 2008 National Transgender Discrimination Survey in the US, 32 per cent had been physically assaulted.

'Did anyone give you a hard time?' Debbie would ask when Sasha got home from school.

The answer was always no. *No, it's fine, I'll be all right.*

One day at a bus stop, an older woman approached Sasha. 'Why are you wearing a skirt?' she demanded. 'You're not a girl!'

'I'm wearing a skirt because I like wearing skirts,' Sasha replied.

That was the worst of it – a single unfriendly question from a woman old enough to be Sasha's grandmother.

Even so, Debbie worried.

Karl was out for a run on Hillegass Avenue, a residential street close to the border between Oakland and Berkeley. It was late November 1987. He was in his early twenties, unmarried, and working at a nearby café. Fugitive scents wisped past his nose as he ran: oak leaves, fog, jasmine, car exhaust, ocean breeze, his own sweat. He was lost in the staccato thud of his shoes hitting the pavement, the huff of his breath, the metronome of his heart.

'Hey, I like your legs!'

A truck slowed down to roll behind him.

Heartbeat louder now, his chest a megaphone. A side-eye peep: three young guys in a pickup truck.

One leaned out the window. 'Let me suck your prick.'

Adrenaline gushed into Karl's veins. He veered down busy Alcatraz Avenue, legs churning. The truck followed. He doubled back to Hillegass, heartbeat pounding out the words of his puzzlement: What do they want from me?

His pursuers threw the truck into reverse and revved past him, slowing down to let one of the men get out. Karl sprinted down a side street. The truck zoomed forward again, following.

Karl's T-shirt was damp with a mélange of different kinds of sweat: heat, effort, fear. Adrenaline kited him down the street.

Then the truck pulled over just in front of him. The driver got out, blocking the pavement. 'Hey, why don't you talk to us?'

Karl halted in midstride. Alarm swamped his ears. 'Because I'm busy,' he choked out.

He didn't even hear the second guy come up behind him.

When he came to, he was lying on the pavement in a circle of concerned bystanders, his head and face aching. The police were on their way. The guys who had attacked him were long gone.

That evening, he wrote about the incident in his journal. *Pretty bizarre*, he commented. He didn't bother ruminating on why he'd been singled out, why the men had assumed he was gay. It was just a random event. A onetime thing. Not likely to be repeated.

All-school meetings at Maybeck are held every Wednesday in the sanctuary of the Presbyterian church downstairs. Students sprawl in the pews to hear musical performances, make announcements, and sometimes hear a guest speaker. One day, in the March of their penultimate year at Maybeck, Sasha mounted the semicircular stage and announced three things:

1. I'm Sasha and I identify as agender.
2. It's important to respect people's preferred pronouns and if you're not sure what those are, you should ask.
3. I'm petitioning the White House to recognise nonbinary gender.

Any US citizen over the age of thirteen can start a petition on the We the People website at Whitehouse.gov, requesting that the government address a problem or change a policy. If a petition gets enough signatures within a thirty-day window, the White House will issue an official response. Sasha's petition read:

> *Legal documents in the United States only recognize "male" and "female" as genders, leaving anyone who does not identify as one of these two genders with no option. Australia and New Zealand both allow an X in place of an M or an F on passports for this purpose, and the UK recognizes 'Mx' (pronounced "Mix") as a gender-neutral title.*
>
> *This petition asks the Obama administration to legally recognize genders outside of the male-female binary, and provide an option for these genders on all legal documents and records.*

To Sasha's astonishment, the petition garnered more than 27,000 signatures. That would have been enough to trigger an official response from the White House were it not for a petition circulated a couple of months earlier asking the White House to build a Death Star like the one in the movie *Star Wars*. After the Death Star petition got more than 34,000 signatures, the White House raised the number of signatures required for an official response from 25,000 to 100,000.

Still, 27,000 signatures wasn't too shabby.

'That was 27,000 people reading and agreeing with my words – words that *I* had written,' Sasha said. 'That felt pretty great.'

CLIPBOARDS

At the end of the school year, Sasha went to Sequoia Elementary School, where Karl worked, to help pack up his kindergarten classroom for the summer. As they boxed up books and folders and unpinned words from the word wall, Sasha noticed the pair of clipboards parents used to sign out their kids at the end of the day. One clipboard was marked *Girls*. The other was marked *Boys*.

'What about the kids who aren't either one?' Sasha asked. 'Which clipboard do *they* go on?'

'It's just a logistical thing,' Karl explained. 'I want to have clipboards on both sides of the door, so there isn't a big line – it's just easier this way.' He couldn't imagine that kindergartners would care about gender one way or the other.

In August, when Karl returned to his classroom to set up for the new school year, he unpacked the clipboards from the box where

Sasha had stowed them. As he hung them up on their hooks by the door, Sasha's comment came back to him. Would it really be that hard to divide things up some other way? Using a black Sharpie, he wrote new labels for the clipboards: *A–M* and *N–Z*. It was a little thing, easy enough to change, he decided.

Three years later, Karl's classroom included a boy who sometimes liked to dress as a princess and a girl who talked about maybe being a boy one day.

'Turned out, Sasha was right,' Karl said. 'Kindergartners don't want to be pigeonholed.'

Best day ever. It was a trademark Sasha phrase. As in, *That was the best day ever!* If you have a lot of obsessions, a lot of things you really like, the opportunity for best days ever increases. On a college visit to the Massachusetts Institute of Technology in Cambridge, US the summer before senior year, Sasha met a fellow fan of the intricately plotted web comic *Homestuck* on a subway platform. The person complimented Sasha's skirt and said, 'I would be wearing mine but it's in the wash.' The two exchanged Tumblr URLs.

Best. Day. Ever.

Because subway. Because Cambridge. Because *Homestuck*. Because Tumblr. Because skirt.

DRESS CODE

Sleek or flouncy
cinched at the waist
pleated, knitted
patterned, plain.

At El Camino Real High School
in 1968, girls wore skirts or
went home.

Pants! Pants!
Let Girls Wear Pants!
Debbie and her friends stood up
on two fabric-swaddled legs
and won.

Still, there were rules.

No jeans. No minis.

Once, Debbie made herself a dress

from an Indian bedspread:

high neck, paisley print

hippie meets granny.

The school sent her home.

That ruffled draping skirt, they said,

was just

too long.

The call to evacuate came about an hour after the students from Maybeck arrived in Yosemite for the school's annual camping trip. It was August 2013, just before the start of Sasha's final year at Maybeck. The Rim Fire, the third-largest wildfire in California history, was sizzling toward the campsite near Groveland, turning the sky a smoky orange. Sasha climbed into the back of a U-Haul-style truck with Nemo, who was a year younger. The truck was airless, hot and cramped.

'We kind of died,' Nemo explained later.

'We didn't *actually* die,' Sasha said.

'We were both freaking out,' Nemo said. 'That was our first date.' The two of them were talking to filmmaker Lonny Shavelson, who was making a documentary film about nonbinary gender called *Three to Infinity*. Nemo identifies as gender fluid.

'To me *gender fluid* means I have the potential to be anything, any gender at any time,' Nemo explained. 'I can be male, female, masculine, feminine, neither, both.' Like Sasha, Nemo uses *they/them* pronouns.

Sasha and Nemo knew each other from the school's Queer Club and had gone to see *Les Misérables* together the year before. But after their ordeal in the back of the evacuation truck, their relationship changed, although neither of them was exactly sure how to define it. Both teenagers were shy and awkward, looking at each other more than at the camera. But they did their best to explain.

'Our relationship is …,' Sasha said.

'Confusing,' Nemo finished.

'It's a platonic relationship,' Sasha said, 'but with elements other people might consider romantic.'

'Cuddling and kissing and stuff,' Nemo added. 'But it's not romantic. It's also nonsexual. It's like, take a regular relationship and instead of kissing, put cuddling and stuff like that. And instead of "I love you's" it's like, "You're the greatest."'

'I'm aromantic,' Sasha explained. 'So I don't really do romantic relationships.'

'And I'm asexual, so I don't do sexual relationships,' Nemo said.

'Our relationship sort of sprang fully-formed on that camping trip, or that fire evacuation,' Sasha added. 'It just started happening. It was like, "Yup, this is it. This is how it works." We sort of stabilise each other. Or complement each other.'

In *Homestuck*, it's called a moirail. A most important person. A soulmate, maybe, but not in the romantic sense. The fact that both of them identified as nonbinary wasn't the reason they were together, it was just another thing they had in common.

PART 2

RICHARD

BOOK OF FACES

(Pictures of Richard posted on Facebook)

Smiling beside his cousin's
slit-eyed hilarity.

Deadpan in ladies'
tortoiseshell sunglasses.

At fourteen, in a beanie:
round-faced, bright-eyed.

At sixteen: jaw slack, brows raised,
expression asking, *What?*

Soft-eyed on a sofa,

younger brother cuddled on his chest.

Standing with Skeet, spines straight,
chins up, peas in a pod.

And later, beside Skeet's picture,
wearing a bandanna in tribute.

Mirror selfie: hand lodged
in his waistband, not even looking up.

None of it captures
how he looks in conversation

how his eyes hold your eyes,
seeing you see him.

His own secret power:
that paying attention.

FIRST DAY

The smell that is the lemon-pine-disinfectant
of just-mopped floors,
that is new jeans still chemical-scented,
pencil shavings, sweat, fryer grease,
body spray, reeking bathrooms, weed
smoke, morning breath—
The smell that is the salty press of bodies changing classes
that is socks that is feet that is blood that is bones
that is finding your way through halls and up stairs
to a classroom filled with unnamed faces—
That smell is the pungent eraser that wipes
the whiteboard clean, so just
ignore the ghosts of last year's scrawl
still there, still showing through.

Cherie couldn't believe it when she saw Richard at Oakland High School. 'Oh my God!' she cried, hugging him. The two of them had grown up in the same apartment building over by Eighty-Seventh Avenue, a two-story, tan-stucco building with a couple of windblown Monterey pines in front. When they were younger, they'd been inseparable, even though they went to different schools. Now they were in their penultimate year of high school, and they hadn't seen each other for more than 12 months.

It had been a terrible year for both of them. They were still broken; maybe they'd never be fixed again. But it was so *good* to see each other. Even depressed and hurting, Cherie sparkled. She was funny, sassy and head-turningly pretty, with creamy brown skin, long straight hair, and a perky, pierced nose. Richard was good-looking too – round-faced and hazel-eyed, with a way of holding your gaze that could make you feel like you were at the centre of the world. He was so light-skinned that people often assumed he was mixed race, and he acted younger than he was –*hyphy*, as they say in Oakland. Always smiling, always joking, always goofing around, whether or not it was the time for it.

'You don't want to be bothered, he'll just keeping talking to you, keep playing, to the point where you'll cuss him out and he'll still be laughing,' Cherie says. 'He likes attention. He likes to bother you. He likes to play hit you, play fight with you. Like, "Leave me alone! Oh my God!"'

Around strangers he was quiet, alert, fading into the background until he was just a pair of hazel eyes watching everything go down. But if you were his friend, then you were family to him. He called you brother or sister, and he'd be loyal until the sun quit rising in the east.

'He got on my nerves but I loved him to death,' Cherie recalls. 'He was my friend. I don't know what I would do without him.'

O High wasn't the best school in Oakland, but it wasn't the worst one either, not by a long shot. It was right in the middle in almost every respect. Perched upslope from downtown, it was high enough on the hill that you could roll a quarter down Park Boulevard and have it land with a splash in Lake Merritt, but not high enough to float above all the regular Oakland drama. Few white families sent their kids there, but every other group did – Asians (44 per cent), African Americans (33 per cent), Latinos (18 per cent). Oakland's open enrolment process allowed families to apply to any school in the district, and Oakland High was a popular choice. Kids travelled from all over the city, north, east and west, leaving behind their neighbourhood skirmishes for a school they hoped might be a little safer, a little saner than the one closer to home. There was a security guard posted at the front gate to keep the craziness out, but there was plenty of craziness to be found inside. Some of it you had to look for, but some of it was hard to ignore – a girl trying to slit her wrists in the bathroom, a fight in the hallway, students shouting, running, sobbing, rumours about who got shot and who hooked up, who was looking for whom and what they'd say when they found them.

You could steer clear of it though. Plenty did. There were AP classes and academies – public health, visual arts, environmental science. There was an African American Male Achievement Program to mentor black boys. There was an on-site Wellness Centre with counselling, health and academic support services. There was football, baseball, basketball, track, as long as you could keep your grades above a certain level.

The finish line was marked with a cap and gown and a march across the stage. That year, two-thirds of O High's students made it. You could get there, if nothing knocked you down. But life had a way of sticking its foot out, sending you sprawling. And then you were part of the other one-third, hanging in the hallways instead of going to class, or just drifting away altogether, away from school, away from that march across the stage, into a future that was as hazy as weed smoke.

Of course, you rarely notice when you come to the fork in the road. It just feels like another day. A day when you didn't go to school because you were sick or your baby sister was sick, or you didn't study for that test so why bother taking it, or your clothes looked ratty and you were tired of hearing about it, or someone was looking for you and you needed to lay low for a few days, or any of a hundred other reasons that made not going to class seem like a better choice than going. Only once you stopped going it just seemed too hard to start again. Days rolled into weeks. Weeks into months. And then at some point you realised you'd entered the future. The one you never planned on. The one where everything was going to be that much harder.

It was three weeks after the start of the 2013–2014 school year and a friend of Richard's was being sent home for fighting. She texted Richard to tell him and he went to meet her at the bus stop. It was still the middle of the day, but he didn't care. He was sixteen now, but back when he and Cherie were fourteen they ditched school all the time, wandering through the city with their friends, looking for fun, courting trouble. He wasn't really in the habit of going to school all day, every day.

But when Richard's friend showed up at the bus stop, she wasn't alone. She was being escorted by a petite woman with long black hair, dangly earrings, and a smile like a flash of sunlight. Her name was Kaprice Wilson, and she was O High's attendance compliance officer. She didn't know Richard, but she knew he was a student and it was the middle of the school day. Richard's friend needed to get on that bus and go home, she said, but Richard needed to get to class.

Richard followed her back to school, peppering her with questions. Who was she, and what did she do? She seemed different from your typical school official. She had a homegirl vibe.

'I'm the truancy coordinator,' Kaprice said. 'And what happens is, if you miss a lot of school, then you're in an intervention programme with me.'

'So you try to help kids that's been in trouble?' Richard asked.

Kaprice nodded.

'Well, that's me,' he said. 'Can I get in your programme?'

Kaprice stared at him. Nobody ever *asked* to join her programme – students were assigned to it after they'd missed so much school they were in danger of flunking out, dropping out, or getting kicked off the roster. She wasn't exactly trying to fill slots either. At a school with 1,875 kids, she had a caseload of some 800 chronically truant students, and if she was lucky she'd be able to work with 275 of them in the course of a year.

'Yeah,' Richard said. "I want you to help me like you help them. Because I've been to a lot of schools and I've been in trouble, but I'm really not a bad kid.'

Back in her office, Kaprice looked up Richard's record. He was already sixteen, and her programme was meant for younger students, who are easier to get back on track. But it was clear he needed help. His grades were poor, his attendance spotty. O High was his third high school in Oakland, plus he'd spent a year living in a group home in Redding, California, three and a half hours away. He'd been placed there by the juvenile authorities after being arrested for fighting when he was a freshman.

Next time they talked, Kaprice told Richard that if he worked with her, he'd have to learn a new set of rules. 'Once you cross over into this lane, you know what you'll be able to get away with?' she asked him.

He shook his head, puzzled. 'What?'

'Nothing. Absolutely nothing. Because I'm going to make you understand the family motto: *Never let your obstacles become more important than your goal.* Right now, your goal is to graduate, and if you don't comply with the family motto, then just know I have a collection of belts in the back of my filing cabinet and they're not for sagging pants.'

Richard laughed. 'I understand,' he said, and grinned.

Kaprice Wilson came of age in East Oakland in the 1980s, when crack cocaine was just hitting the streets. For users, crack meant poverty – whole lives stripped down like a stolen car, the parts sold off to pay for their next hit. But for dope dealers, crack meant power and respect, fat wads of paper money, gold chains and gaudy jewellery, fancy cars.

'Everything was in the moment,' Kaprice says. 'No one thought about how it would affect our children.'

When she was fourteen she saw a boy on a bike playing chicken with a car at the corner of Eighty-Second Avenue and MacArthur Boulevard. The boy rode up close to the car, trying to freak out the driver. The driver swerved and tried to hit him. The boy on the bike dodged away and crashed into the kerb, jumping over the bike and landing on his feet, grinning.

'Damn, did y'all see that?' he asked. 'He almost hit me.'

His name was Lil' Jerry and he was thirteen. Kaprice fell for him on the spot. The regard was mutual. Soon they were talking on the phone every night. When Kaprice went to his house for the first time, his sisters told her Lil' Jerry wouldn't stop talking about her. That's how she knew she was his girlfriend.

Lil' Jerry had been 'claiming' East Oakland's 69vill gang since he was five or six years old. He'd started out earning petty cash by ironing and rubber-banding wrinkled money from dice games, and then moved up in the organisation. But even after he grew up to be six feet two, he was still known as Lil' Jerry. By the age of fifteen he was carrying around backpacks full of money. Too young to have a driver's license, he was already wealthy enough to own four or five cars. He liked to go to Las Vegas to watch the fights wearing fur boxers and a long mink coat.

69vill was led by Felix Mitchell, who controlled much of the West Coast heroin market. He was arrested in 1983 and sentenced to life in prison two years later. Fourteen months after that, he was stabbed to death by a fellow prisoner. His funeral made the national news, the coffin conducted through the streets of Oakland on a horse-drawn carriage followed by a procession of four Rolls-Royces, ten white limousines and an assortment of Cadillacs and Lincolns. Thousands of Oaklanders lined the streets to watch the eight-mile parade. Kaprice's mother wouldn't let her go. She didn't know that it was too late to worry about Mitchell's bad example.

Violence skyrocketed after Mitchell's death as other gangsters battled for a piece of his turf as well as the increasingly lucrative crack trade. Year by year, the number of murders climbed steadily

– from 114 in 1987 to 165 in 1992. The corpses weren't evenly distributed throughout the city, though. They were clustered on the east and west sides of town. East Oakland in particular was awash with crack, blood and bullets.

Kaprice was living too fast a life to stay at home, so she moved in with her stepsister's family. One of the girls' chores was to clean the guns. When boys came over, Kaprice and her stepsister would be sitting at a table with brush, rod and cloth, expertly taking the guns apart, spinning the barrels, polishing the grips. A visitor would have to be pretty slow not to get the message: these girls were not to be messed with.

Lil' Jerry called her Kaprice Classic, after the car. (He owned one of those too.) She got a bit part in a Jim Belushi movie called *The Principal* and Lil' Jerry called her a movie star. She knew everybody, and everybody knew of her – Lil' Jerry Cooper's beautiful, smart-alecky girlfriend. 'By the time I got to be eighteen or nineteen, I thought I was like the Princess of East Oakland,' she says. 'Because 69vill was the gang that had all the hype. It was the most feared.'

Kaprice's brother went off to college in Atlanta, but Kaprice had no interest. She'd tried junior college, but couldn't be bothered to do more than cash the financial aid cheque. When her brother handed her an application pack for Clark Atlanta University, she threw it away. No way was she giving up her East Oakland status just to go to school.

Then an acceptance letter arrived in the mail. Her brother had filled out the application for her and mailed it in.

'You're going,' Lil' Jerry said when she told him.

But Kaprice had another plan. She wanted to get pregnant. She knew she and Jerry would have beautiful children together.

'How are you going to support a baby?' Lil' Jerry asked.

Kaprice shrugged. 'I'll go on welfare.' That's what all the girls she knew did.

'You sound so stupid right now,' Lil' Jerry said. 'You know what's going to happen? They're going to kill me. And I do not want to have a baby out here without a dad. I don't want that for you and I don't want that for my child. There will be enough of those kids out there. You can take those ones in. Just know that those ones will be your and my children together, and when they get crazy and out of control, help them. Because they're going to need help.'

Lil' Jerry refused to sleep with her after that. 'He froze me,' Kaprice says. 'He was like, "You're not messing with nobody else either. Try somebody else, I'll kill them and I'll kill you first."'

So she went to college. She majored in education. Ran track and got an athletic scholarship. Won an award for student teacher of the year from the dean of the school of education. Once, when she came home during a break, she learned that Lil' Jerry had been shot three times. She heard it from a friend – he hadn't told her, didn't want her to know. But when she held his hand, she could feel a bullet lodged beneath the skin.

It was clear the thug life was wearing him down – the violence, the danger, the vigilance. 'We just need to stop the madness,' he would say. 'Just stop the madness.' He drank too much, smoked too much weed. He began dressing like he was a blue-collar worker – jackets from UPS and Home Depot, a back brace like he had a job in a warehouse. He was twenty-four years old – in their world, that made him practically an old man.

One day he got into a conversation with an elderly woman who lived on Eighty-Ninth Avenue, a couple of blocks from his house. She wouldn't go outside because of all the drug dealing in the neighbourhood, but she told him she wished she could have flowers in her front garden. He bought her some and planted them himself. Put a little gate around them so they wouldn't get trampled by the customers going to the house next door to buy drugs. Paid attention every time he passed her house on the way to the store. Which is why he had to say something when he saw one of those drug customers take a shortcut across the garden.

'Man, did you see the fence was there?' he asked. 'Why would you walk across the flowers? Just walk around. She growing some flowers.'

'I don't give a fuck about them flowers,' the guy said. He didn't know who Lil' Jerry was. Just some guy in a puffy jacket.

'Why you got to be like that? Just respect her flowers.'

Now it was a challenge. '*Fuck* them flowers,' the guy said. 'I'ma come back and shoot this shit up.'

And he did. Or someone did. Within hours, Lil' Jerry was gunned down on the pavement. Kaprice had left just a few minutes before. She'd been talking to Lil' Jerry about what she was going to make for dinner. He said it sounded good. She'd promised to save him some.

Afterward, two things stuck in her mind. One was how neat the shooting had been. It wasn't one of the ones where blood went everywhere. There wasn't even a stain on the pavement.

The other was how nobody on the block saw who did it. It wasn't like they were pretending they hadn't seen, the way people did when they didn't want to get involved. It was more like that bit from the *Men in Black* movies, where bystanders have their memories erased.

It seemed to Kaprice like Lil' Jerry must have wanted it that way. 'I don't want anybody to retaliate,' she imagined him saying. 'I just want to leave. I'm ready.'

The killing, like so many in East Oakland, was never solved.

'That experience – it really grew me up and taught me a lot about life,' she said, twenty years after Lil' Jerry's murder. 'Just appreciating the moment. And doing the most you can do, you know, to help somebody else.'

Within a year she had her first job as a school teacher in East Oakland. The troublesome kids kept getting sent her way – the ones who had been kicked out of other classrooms. She knew these kids, or she knew kids like them, and she knew how to work with them. They were her children, just like Lil' Jerry had said.

At Oakland High School, Kaprice served as a surrogate mum to the kids who needed one the most – the ones who had trouble just getting to school every day. Some of them, like Cherie, even called her Mom, bringing her their grades, photographs and artwork to hang on her walls and writing her apologies when they ran into trouble. Her tiny office was papered with their missives:

From son Oscar, I ♥ you mom, read one.

I'm sorry mom, she made me hecka mad, said another – written by a girl who had just been suspended for fighting.

Kaprice taught her kids to look out for one another, even when their inclination was to squabble. If a student wanted to be one of her children, they had to accept that they were gaining siblings as well as a mother.

'We're family,' she told them. 'This is your sister. This is your brother. You have no say in the matter.' On her walls she'd posted the family slogan: *Never let your obstacles become more important than your goal.*

The goals: go to class, get your grades up, graduate, stay out of jail, survive.

Her office was a safe zone for Richard. It was the size of a walk-in cupboard, tucked off a hallway near the main office, but it had a sofa where kids could sit and talk, take a breath, regroup, relax. He'd drop in between lessons just to touch base.

'He never wanted to get out of her office,' Cherie remembers. 'I mean, he really loved her.' Cherie was already one of Kaprice's children – Kaprice had helped her get off probation the year before, and she had never caught another case. Before long, Richard asked if he could call Kaprice Mom too, but she wouldn't let him. He already had a mum he was close to – she wasn't going to try to take that spot.

'I'll be your auntie,' she told him.

Richard's mother, Jasmine, was already four and a half months pregnant when her grandmother took her to the doctor to get checked. She was fourteen years old and had been dating a boy two years older. He was the one who figured out she was pregnant – she hadn't known enough to make sense of the changes happening to her body. It was too late for an abortion, but Jasmine figured she was prepared to raise a child. She loved babysitting her niece and nephew. How hard could it be?

'I thought it was about dressing them up and buying them clothes,' she recalled.

Richard was born the summer before Jasmine turned fifteen. She split up with his father eleven months later. Richard still saw him frequently over the years, or as frequently as he could given that his father was sometimes in prison for drug offences. When Richard was five, Jasmine got involved with a new man, Derick. Richard was resentful, still holding out hope that his parents would get back together. 'You're not my dad,' he told Derick.

Being a mother was harder than Jasmine had expected, but she took pains to do it well. Richard's temperament made it easier – he was a happy kid, always dancing and singing, playful and silly. She brought him to church every Sunday, taught him to recite his prayers and say grace before he ate, made sure he held the door open for women and seniors, minded his manners, was helpful around the house. Richard's friends knew his mum ran a tight ship – no disrespect, no talking back.

Jasmine had two sisters, Juliette and Savannah, each of whom had children of their own. The three sisters were young and beautiful, with high foreheads, large, almond-shaped eyes, and full, Cupid's-bow lips. There was always a lot of laughing when they were together. The kids moved easily among the sisters' houses cocooned in the warmth of a large extended family.

But on 30 December 30 2006, when Richard was nine years old, everything changed. A car parked in San Francisco was sprayed with bullets, killing three people inside. Savannah was one of them. She left behind two little girls, aged four and eleven. They moved in with Richard, Jasmine and Derick. Jasmine treated her nieces as daughters, but it was hard on everyone. The girls had lost their mother. Jasmine had lost her sister. And nine-year-old Richard had gone from being the centre of his mother's world to just one more traumatised member of a family with a gaping hole in it.

'I don't get any attention now,' he told his mum.

Jasmine tried to explain. 'I know how *I* feel because it was my sister. You know how *you* feel because it was your auntie. But for them it was their *mom*. And I have to share the love, you know? Even it out.'

Two years later, Jasmine had a baby with Derick. The household now had six members: Derick and Jasmine, Richard and his new brother, Derriyon, plus the two girls. They had moved into a four-bedroom stucco bungalow in the far reaches of East Oakland's Elmhurst neighborhood. The house was pale pink and had rosebushes in the front garden. It was a tough neighbourhood, but a quiet street.

Jasmine had always hoped to continue her education. But it was a scramble just to get the bills paid and the children cared for and the house scrubbed and neat the way she liked it, no spots on the glass tabletop, no dust in the corners. When Richard was at high school, she was working in food service at a residential care facility. She wanted something better for Richard. 'I'm not making that much at my job,' she said. 'I want him to have a *career*. Go to college.' She hadn't saved much, but she figured if he started out at community college, he could transfer to a state university.

These were big dreams in her part of town. Of the roughly six hundred African American boys who started Oakland high schools each year, only about three hundred ended up graduating. Fewer than one hundred graduated with the requirements needed to attend a California state college or university.

The odds of landing in the back of a police car, on the other hand, were much better. African American boys made up less than 30 per cent of Oakland's underage population but accounted for nearly 75 per cent of all juvenile arrests.

Jasmine worried about Richard. Prayed. Prayed he'd graduate from high school. Prayed he wouldn't become a parent as early as she had. Prayed he'd be safe from all the dangers that lurked for a young black man in Oakland – guns and crime and gangs and cops. Prayed he'd stay out of trouble. Prayed he'd survive.

Richard brought Kaprice his schoolwork to put up on the wall, just like the others did. His grades weren't great, but that wasn't the point. Getting a D was better than getting an F. 'Next time it'll be a C,' she told him. 'Before long it'll be a B. And then you'll be making straight As.'

When the two of them were alone, he confided in her about his life, replaying things that had happened and explaining how he'd do them differently now. Sometimes he'd tell her about a situation he was struggling with and ask for advice. But most of the time they weren't alone. Kaprice had a lot of other children. When they were in the office, Richard sat and listened to them talk.

'He would make himself invisible, but he would observe and notice everything,' Kaprice says. 'A lot of times, students would come in here and he was like their little counsellor. He would help them get through whatever was going on.'

He wanted people to be happy, that was the thing everybody

noticed about him. He was always joking, goofing around. Kaprice had a toy basketball hoop on her door to give her students' younger siblings something to do when their parents came in for meetings. She usually kept it pinned up so the bigger kids wouldn't use it, because when they did things tended to get out of hand. Richard would shoot balled-up paper through it on the sly, making sure Kaprice noticed. 'Did you see that bird, Miss Kaprice?'

If the mood in the room was tense he might suddenly pull his trousers up high above his waist like a nerd to get people giggling.

'There's already enough craziness,' he told Kaprice. 'I just like happy stuff.'

That's how everyone knew Richard – as the funny one, the one who made people smile. He pulled pranks like putting ketchup on people's faces while they slept, or ambushing them with water balloons when they'd just woken up. He would do anything for a laugh – put on one of his female cousins' sexy cropped sweaters, for example, or post a selfie on Instagram of himself dressed in a bra and a wig, gazing into the bathroom mirror with a sultry expression. *I'm a THOT for Halloween*, the caption explained.

That autumn, Jasmine was planning a family trip to Disneyland.

'You might not have fun because you're a big kid now,' she told Richard.

That wouldn't be a problem, he assured her. 'I'm going to have fun like I'm five years old.'

He'd lost a year of his childhood, his cousin Gerald pointed out later. He'd only just come back after being sent away. 'He didn't really get to experience the fun time. He's probably, like, living from where he left off.'

Sometimes when Cherie thinks about her old friends, her eyes fill up with tears. 'I'm not going to say we were angels,' she says. 'I'm not going to say we were scholars. But we all had good hearts. We looked out for each other because that was all we knew.' She was talking about 2012, the year she and Richard were freshmen in high school, before everything went bad. In those days they cut school on the daily, heading to the intersection of Fruitvale Avenue and MacArthur Boulevard, where kids gathered from all over town in the afternoons to talk and flirt and play dice, occasionally to fight.

They had a crew they called the Heartbreak Kidz, not a gang but a play gang, a set of initials to write down in jagged letters: *HBK*. They went bowling. They went to the beach. They rode the bus all over town, stopping in at high schools where they didn't even go to school, just to visit whoever might be hanging around the halls. They knew everyone, it seemed, everyone from the east side anyway, but they loved one another best. They'd grown up together, and now they were in high school, full of sass and fire. Skeet and Ashley were the oldest, at sixteen. Jesse was fifteen. Cherie, Hadari and Dae were fourteen. So was Richard, though he seemed younger.

'Skeet used to take up for him,' Cherie remembered. 'Richard was like a little brother, he was the youngest one. Him and Hadari but Hadari, he brave-hearted, he didn't take too much from nobody. But Richard, like, everybody just watch him. Richard's hecka goofy and hecka obnoxious, and would do something stupid. He would do the craziest stuff.'

Back then they had their whole lives ahead of them, or so they thought. It wasn't supposed to turn out like it did, which is why the tears keep leaking from her eyes as she talks. She never dreamed it would turn out like it did.

Because at the time?

At the time they were beautiful, they were young, and they had one another. And it was fun. Not gonna lie – in those days it was hecka fun.

They wanted to go to the beach. It wasn't particularly warm, maybe 20°C, if that, but they were bored and so they went – Richard, Cherie, Dae, Skeet, Hadari, Jesse and Ashley, all of them on the bus to the beach. It was April 2012. The way Cherie remembers it, they got off at Fruitvale to change buses but Ashley wasn't paying attention.

'Ashley! Come on! *Ashley!* We finna miss the bus!'

Turns out there was another girl on the bus named Ashley. She and her friend got off the bus behind them.

'Why y'all following us?' Ashley demanded. 'What y'all want?'

That was just what they did in those days. Argued.

Now Ashley and Other Ashley were arguing, and Dae was arguing with Other Ashley's friend.

'Come on,' Cherie called. 'They don't want no problems.' The argument seemed pointless to her. Stupid. They were trying to get to the beach.

But then, according to Cherie, Ashley hit Other Ashley, and the fight began for real. Cherie tried to break it up and got hit, so she hit back. Then Richard tried to break it up, but he got hit too. In the tussle that followed, something fell out of Other Ashley's bag – insulin and needles. Richard picked them up and tried to hand them to her, but she threw them at him, and so they all just took off, laughing and breathless.

'She was so hyphy!'

'Why'd she have all them needles?'

'She must have diabetes.'

'I tried to give it back to her. Oh well.'

They ended up in a park, Cherie remembers. Scrubby grass, a football field, tennis courts. There were some Latino kids there, skateboarders. How the boys ended up fighting them was a mystery to Cherie, but that's what happened. Somebody spoke to somebody wrong and then Skeet and Hadari were fighting, and Richard joined in because if his friends were fighting, he'd fight too. Skeet hit one of the kids with a skateboard.

'It was hecka savage,' Cherie said later.

Then they went to the beach. Ran around in the sand, talked about what had happened. Partied. Adrenaline pumping. Laughing. Bleeding a little.

On the way home, the bus went down Fruitvale. Looking through the windows, they saw the girls they'd fought with, and the skateboarders from the park. 'Look, there they are! They're talking to the police!'

Then a police car pulled up behind the bus.

'**We were just young,**' Cherie explained. 'We didn't even think we could go to jail for it. Honestly, we didn't think about jail when it happened.'

But the law didn't see it that way. The police arrested Richard, Cherie, Dae, Skeet, Hadari and Ashley. Jesse had already got off the bus by then, so he got away. The rest of them kept waiting to go home, but they weren't allowed to go home.

Juvenile offender records are sealed, so it's impossible to reconstruct exactly what went down. But it appears that the skateboarders said some of their stuff was missing, including a cell phone. Nothing was found on Richard and his friends, but charges were brought. Sometime after midnight they were booked into Juvenile Hall. That's where they stayed, distributed across separate units. Juvenile Hall policy doesn't let kids who are arrested together stay together, both so they don't have a chance to compare stories and to keep them from getting into any more trouble.

The first time they went to court, for a detention hearing, Richard got all goofy, excited to be reunited with his friends, sure that when the court appearance was over they would get to go home. But that's not what happened. There's no bail for juvenile offenders – it's up to the judge to decide whether to let you go home or keep you in custody. When there's violence involved, they tend to keep you. Hadari had known. He was the only one of them who'd ever been arrested before. He said, 'We're not getting out of jail. Don't even think that.'

And he was right. Cherie recalls that they were in custody for a time and then one by one they went their separate ways. Cherie got out on probation, a GPS monitor on her ankle. Skeet and Hadari were sentenced to out-of-home placement and sent to group homes, where they would have to complete formal treatment programmes before returning to their families. Richard was released on GPS early on, but eventually he was sentenced to a group home in Redding, California, a three-and-a-half-hour drive from Oakland. He would stay there until the following summer, more than a year after his arrest.

The six kids would never all be together again. After that, everything went wrong instead of right.

Skeet was an extrovert, a goofball, a practical joker. People remembered him after they met him. They remembered his quick wit, his energy, his magnetism, his loyalty and – if they got on the wrong side of it – his temper. He was the one who could do a backflip off a traffic barrier. The one who sauntered on and off the debate team at Skyline High School, sometimes showing up, sometimes not, but always quick on his feet, leading with his wit and his gift of the gab, even if he couldn't be bothered with the preparation.

Skeet was sent to Boys Republic, a residential treatment facility for troubled youths in Chino Hills, California. It's not clear how long he was supposed to stay there, but he ran away and returned to Oakland long before his time was up. On 26 November 2012, he posted a sepia-toned photo of himself on Facebook. He was sitting in a car, head tilted back to look down at the camera, his eyes hooded. He had a gun in his right hand.

What is that, someone queried.

Tre eight, Skeet wrote, meaning that it was a .38-caliber revolver, *but this old b4 I wen tto jail.*

U out foe good?

To myself yeah but to the polce they wannt a nigga.

He'd run away from the group home and was back in Oakland. The day before he posted the gun photo, he'd posted a photo of himself with a bottle of cognac and a bottle of cough syrup. *Got my syrup and my Remy now its a good day.* Now he posted a picture of himself drinking straight from the bottle. *Big Boi Drinking.*

That was his last Facebook post.

On the afternoon of 7 January 2013, more than a month after running away from the group home, he was shot multiple times while driving a car near Hegenberger Road and Hamilton Street. He was seventeen years old. The man police blame for his murder was killed four days later in an outbreak of violence that left four people dead in one six-hour period.

When Richard heard about his friend's death, he called his mother from the group home in Redding to find out if it was true. When she said it was, he began to cry and couldn't stop.

He didn't even hang up. Just put the phone down and walked away.

IF

Everything turned dark then.

Skeet dead.

Skeet dead.

Skeet dead.

'That killed Richard,' Cherie said later. 'It killed all of us.'

She didn't have an explanation for his murder, except the usual: wrong place, wrong time, wrong company. Skeet was two years older than she and Richard were. After he ran away from his southern California group home, he took up with other, more dangerous friends. 'I keep thinking,' Cherie says, 'if we'd never got into that fight, maybe Skeet would still be alive.'

It was an open-casket funeral. Cherie says she almost passed out when she saw Skeet lying dead in his coffin. People had to hold her up.

But at least she wasn't alone. Richard, in a group home three and a half hours away, had no one beside him to keep him from falling. No one who knew Skeet. No one who understood.

MURDER

In 2012, Oakland was the most dangerous city in California. According to Oakland Police Department statistics, there were nearly 2,800 assaults and more than 4,100 robberies. In all, 131 people were killed. Eight of them were under eighteen.

Lamont Price. Killed 16 February 2012. Age 17.
Shot.

Charles Hill III. Killed 23 March 2012. Age 16.
Shot.

Shonte Daniels Jr. Killed 21 April 2012. Age 15.
Shot.

Hadari Askari. Killed 10 July 2012. Age 15.
Shot.

Tattiaunn Turner. Killed 8 August 2012. Age 16.
Shot.

Bobbie Sartain. Killed 25 November 2012. Age 16.
Shot.

Raquel Gerstel. Killed 25 November 2012. Age 15.
Shot.

Jubrille Jordan. Killed 30 December 2012. Age 15.
Shot.

Richard and Cherie didn't know the Hadari who was killed, but they were friends with Charles Hill. He was killed at a party out by Sixty-Eighth Avenue. Cherie was there the night it happened, but she'd been spooked by all the guns at the party and left. She could feel death in the air. She walked down to the corner and called Dae in tears. 'Come get me,' she pleaded. 'Somebody's about to die.' By the time Dae arrived, Charles was dead.

Skeet was the first murder of 2013. There would be another ninety-one people killed before the year was out. Seven of the people who were shot were younger than eighteen, including an eight-year-old girl and a sixteen-month-old boy.

'Every year we lose somebody,' Cherie says. 'It's just like, who's next? I'm scared for myself because bullets don't have no names on them. That's why I don't go outside. There's too much going on.'

Richard had lost two aunts to murder – his mother's sister Savannah and his father's sister, Tish, who was killed by her boyfriend in 2008. Now he'd lost two of his friends. Violence was like the fog that swept in from San Francisco Bay on summer afternoons to cloak the city in damp shadow. Even in the bright sunshine, you knew it could roll in at any minute and chill you to the bone.

Richard returned to Oakland the following summer, having spent an entire year in Redding. Jasmine was delighted to have him home. She'd visited him regularly while he was away and talked with him on the phone, but it had been hard on both of them. Now it was time for a fresh start. Richard signed up for a job-training programme conducted by the Unity Council, an Oakland not-for-profit organisation, which led to an internship. The workshop facilitator, Josue Guzman, noticed that Richard stood out from the other young participants. He was smart and focused and a quick learner, and he seemed to be enjoying himself.

Richard loved having a job. He was conscientious about arriving promptly, and he took care with his work, doing things right the first time and stepping in to fix mistakes made by other interns. Once, Guzman asked Richard to help him with a project another intern hadn't completed, organising some notes Guzman had jotted down on a notepad about the summer workshop and turning them into an organised lesson plan. Richard took the scattered, out-of-order notes, typed them, and arranged them into easy-to-follow lessons. Guzman was impressed.

Richard really did amazing work during his internship, he wrote in a letter. *I am confident when I say that he has the potential to achieve anything that he wants.*

Jasmine noticed how much more grown-up Richard seemed now that he was working. He offered to help out with the bills instead of spending his earnings on himself. He liked being a man with a paycheck.

STRIPPED

It was the end of October, two months into Richard's penultimate year of high school. He and his cousin Gerald were on their way over to Cherie's house to kick it with her brother and they stopped in at a liquor store to get something to drink. That's when Richard ran into a boy he knew from around the way.

A few minutes later: two guns to his head.

Gerald was walking in front, so he didn't see what happened. But suddenly Richard wasn't wearing his pink Nike Foamposites anymore. Richard's face was crimson, the way it always got when he was furious.

In Oakland it's called getting stripped. The kid took his wallet, money, phone, shoes, coat. Gerald wanted to go back, find the kids who did it, but Richard told him to keep walking.

He'd been caught without his people, that's all there was to say. But at least he hadn't been killed. Rumour was that the boy who robbed him had killed people.

TRUST ISSUES

Who in this world can you trust?
When the guns are drawn,
when the sun goes down,
when you're walking in the shadows,
Who
      Can
            You
                  Trust?
People call themselves your friend.
They say they were there
      but they weren't there.
Say they're coming
      but they don't show.
Say they got your back

as they get their knives out.
Two tongues in their mouths,
the one they use to promise
and the one they use to lie.
'I don't have any friends,' Richard once said.
'I have associates.'

RESOLVE

After he was robbed, Richard didn't come to school for a few days. When he returned, he sat in Kaprice's office and told her what had happened. He seemed pensive and a little shaken. The whole time the guns were pointed at him, he said, he'd stayed calm. Observing. Trying to figure out how not to have the situation escalate. How not to die.

Then Richard gave Kaprice his mother's phone number.

'The type of character you have and the type of character my mama has, you could almost be friends,' he said.

Kaprice laughed. 'Richard, you know if I become friends with your mom and I'm working here at school, that means she's going to know every single thing that you're doing, because I'm going to tell her.'

'I want you to do that,' Richard said. 'Because I already have a bad rap and I want her to know that I'm really trying to do everything I can to not be like that. I'ma graduate. And I'ma make her happy.'

PART 3

THE FIRE

A week or so after Richard was robbed, Jasmine came into his room to talk to him as he got ready for school.

She was concerned about his schoolwork. He complained sometimes that his classes didn't make sense. Now she told him he needed to talk to his teachers.

'You have to ask for help,' she said.

That afternoon, Richard's cousin Lloyd came by Oakland High looking for him. A heavy, bespectacled kid with a gap between his front teeth, Lloyd was goofy and boisterous – qualities that made him unpopular with the school's security staff. He was two years older than Richard, but he didn't act it.

'Just a big old baby,' campus security officer Carlitta Collins says. 'A big rambunctious ball of energy. I always make Lloyd leave whenever I see him here.'

Richard and Lloyd were always together. Lloyd spent a lot of time at Richard's house, since his own mother was often out of town. Richard looked up to him. 'He would always be with him,' Lloyd's brother Gerald remembers. 'It was just Lloyd and Richard. He was always following behind Lloyd.'

That afternoon, Lloyd wanted Richard to leave school early, but Richard wouldn't do it. So Lloyd hung around outside the gates until Richard was out of school.

''Bye, Auntie,' Richard said to Collins as he left. He opened his arms and gave her a hug.

'He's a beautiful young man,' Collins said later. 'I'm telling you, I didn't feel nothing but love when he hugged me.'

THE 57 BUS

Sasha's bus ride to and from Maybeck High School took an hour and involved as many as two transfers, but Sasha didn't mind. They had always loved the bus. Loved the intersecting lines of routes on the map, the crisp procession of times on the schedule. In their spare time, they drew maps of new bus, subway and tram lines, or read up on historical public transport systems.

'Sasha loves buses in a way I can't even understand,' explains Healy. 'I don't even like buses. They *love* buses. They like *reading* things about buses. You can offer them a ride home and they're like, "I'll take the bus."'

Most days after school, Sasha and their best friend, Michael, walked together from Maybeck to the BART station on College Avenue, about a mile away. Along the way, they'd pass a manhole cover on which someone had spray-painted DO NOT EAT THIS!

Usually, one of them would point out the instruction to the other. 'Hey – don't eat that.'

Most of the time they split up when they got to the BART station. Michael would take the BART train and Sasha would take the bus. Sometimes when they arrived at the station, the train would already be there.

'Dude, I got this,' Michael always said, a joking reference to the impossibility of sprinting upstairs to the platform in time to catch the train. It didn't really make sense. It just seemed funny. They weren't really 'dude'-type people.

After that, Sasha would walk across the street to pick up the first of two buses that would take them home. The 57 was the second. In the afternoon, it was usually packed with students of all ages from a dozen different schools. On game days, the kids from rival high schools razzed each other back and forth. It was loud, obnoxious. Rowdy. The kids were tired, wired, just sprung from school. The adults looked out of the window or studied their phones. Tried not to make eye contact. The bus felt charged with daredevil energy. Hot. Muggy and musky with adolescent bodies.

The first question you faced when getting on was where to sit. Up front, close to the driver? It felt safer there, if the chaos made you nervous. That's where girls tended to sit. In the back, out of sight? More room to spread out. You might even get a seat to yourself.

Sasha liked the back of the bus. A platform seat they could spread out on, tuck their legs under. There they could read, do homework, nap. They had trained themself to wake as the bus rounded the sharp S-curve just before their stop. On 4 November they were unusually tired, having stayed up late the night before writing an essay for their Russian Lit class. Less than twenty-four hours earlier, they'd shared their exhaustion on Tumblr:

> *Do u ever just get rly tired when u have a lot of shit to do and u just start crying for no reason*

Now, as the 57 bus rattled up MacArthur Boulevard, Sasha's eyes drifted closed.

In Oakland, every AC Transit bus is equipped with cameras that continuously record sound and video from multiple vantage points. The 57 bus was no exception. The cameras recorded Lloyd and Richard climbing on at the front a little before five p.m. and walking down the aisle towards the back – Lloyd chubby in a zipped-up black hoodie, Richard lean in a black hoodie over a white T-shirt and an orange-billed New York Knicks hat.

The bus was a double-length one, two buses fused together like conjoined twins by an accordion-pleated rubber seam. Most of the seats were taken. An older woman who wanted to talk to the bus driver about her route. A mum holding the hand of a little girl in a pink hoodie. A gaggle of laughing teenage boys.

'How's everything?' the driver asked a middle-aged man as he slid his bus pass into the machine.

'Long day,' the man replied, shaking his head.

Richard recognised a boy named Jamal sitting at the back of the bus and greeted him with a dap.

'Mali B!' Lloyd shouted, following suit.

'What's up, dude?' Jamal was tall and lanky. He wore jeans and a white hoodie with a thick horizontal black stripe across the shoulders. His voice was low and thick, faded.

As the bus started up again, the two cousins gripped the silver pole in front of Jamal. Behind them, Sasha slept. A paperback copy of *Anna Karenina* lay closed in their lap. Their skirt, gauzy and white, dangled over the edge of the seat.

It couldn't have been easy to sleep with Lloyd nearby. He bounced up and down trying to make the bus shake, rapped a snippet of the song *Started from the Bottom* by Drake, screeched random words like 'Chinchilla!' and 'Obituary!' He shouted down the aisle to a girl he'd noticed when they climbed on board, 'Hey! Girl! Excuse me!'

A girl in blue basketball shorts turned to look at him.

'No, your friend, the light-skinned one.'

Jamal pointed at Sasha, whispered, 'Look at this dude.'

Lloyd turned and looked over his shoulder. He cackled.

On the video, you can't hear what Jamal says as he hands Richard the lighter. But you can see him take out his iPhone and point it towards Sasha as if planning to record. Later Richard would say that it was supposed to be funny, like that prank show on MTV with Ashton Kutcher, *Punk'd*. He thought the fabric would smoulder for a minute and then Sasha would wake up and slap it out, startled.

'I *need* a good laugh,' he'd said just after getting on the bus. Now he showed the lighter to Lloyd and then swung to the opposite side of the silver pole, closer to Sasha.

He flicked the lighter by the hem of Sasha's skirt. Nothing happened.

Lloyd was still shouting up to the front of the bus.

'Hey! Light-skinned girl!'

'Light-skinned girl.' Jamal kept repeating what Lloyd said, his deep voice like an echo from the bottom of a well.

Lloyd bounced up the aisle to where the girls were sitting, perching on the edge of a nearby seat.

'Go ahead, you do it,' Jamal said to Richard. Richard flicked the lighter again. Nothing.

Rebuffed by the girls, Lloyd returned to his companions, stopping in front of Sasha's sleeping form to shout an abrupt, parrotlike 'Hey!'

Sasha stirred, but didn't wake.

'Whoa, nigga. You said, "Hey!"' Jamal echoed. 'Screamin' and shit.'

Lloyd leaned close and screeched in Jamal's ear. Richard laughed and slapped Lloyd's head.

'Aw, nigga, you just broke my neck,' Lloyd yelled. 'Damn, pussy, bitch, fuck!'

Richard brandished the lighter, pretending to light Lloyd's sleeve. He looked at Jamal.

'Do it,' Jamal urged.

Lloyd danced between them, landing half on Jamal's lap.

'Move, nigga! Get off me,' Jamal grumbled. He kept his eyes on Richard, his phone poised. 'You might as well do it,' he said again.

Richard slunk back to Sasha, flicked the lighter. Nothing. He glanced at Jamal, grinned, and flicked the lighter a fourth time.

'Back door! Back door!' Lloyd called to the driver, ready for them to make their escape.

The doors opened. Richard leaped off the bus. Lloyd started to follow. Then he looked back and stopped, transfixed, as Sasha's skirt erupted into a sheet of flame. When the doors closed again, he hadn't moved.

The next few seconds of the surveillance video are hard to watch.

Sasha leaps up, slapping the flaming skirt. 'Oh, fuck! Oh, fuck!' The skirt looks unearthly, impossible, a ball of white fire.

'Ow! *Ow!*' Sasha screams, voice high and terrified. *'I'm on fire! I'm on fire!'* Their hands snatch at the skirt, shaking it, waving it. Specks of flaming fabric swirl through the air. Sasha runs for the door and finds it closed. They turn, dance in place, screaming.

Jamal howls with laughter. Then, as Sasha careens toward him, he cringes and climbs on to his seat. 'He's on fire!' he yells. 'Put him out!'

Passengers sprint for the exits, shrieking and coughing. 'It's a fire! It's a fire!' Some of the other kids on the bus are giggling. The bus is still moving, the driver just starting to register that something is going on way back at the far end of his vehicle.

'I ain't got time to be playin' with y'all, man,' he calls over his shoulder.

Near the middle of the bus, two men leap from their seats and elbow through the press of people trying to escape. One man is short and balding; the other is taller, with a walrusy moustache and sad basset-hound eyes.

'Get down!' the moustached one yells. 'Get on the ground!' The two men don't know each other, but they work in unison, shoving Sasha to the floor. The moustached man smothers Sasha's flaming skirt with his coat while the balding man stamps out the burning tatters that flame around them.

It's over in seconds. The driver pulls the bus to the kerb. Sasha scrambles to a standing position, dazed and in shock. 'Oh, Lord. Fuck.'

'That boy was on *fire*, wasn't he?' a man remarks as Sasha pushes through the back doors to the pavement. Behind him, Sasha's moustached rescuer paces the aisle. 'Call an ambulance,' he croaks. He goes to the door of the bus and calls to Sasha, who roams the pavement with a mobile phone, charred legs. 'You need to call an ambulance, man.'

The girl in the blue basketball shorts calls to Sasha through the doors of the bus. 'Are you OK?'

Sasha doesn't answer.

The bus empties out. Passengers climb off, shaking their heads.

'That don't make no sense. That's really damn sad.'

'See how he burned all up?'

'Oh my God. Who would want to *do* some shit like that?'

'Aw, they got him messed up.'

'That's fucked up. That's *hella* fucked up!'

Then the driver walks down the aisle to the back of the bus and kicks the charred remnant of Sasha's skirt through the door.

'Real stupid motherfuckers, man!' he bellows.

WATCHING

After he jumped off the bus, Richard strode away with his hands in his pockets, trying to look casual. Then he heard Sasha's screams. He stopped, turned around, went back.

He stared at the bus, mouth open.

The bus had begun to move again. The driver, still unaware of the fire, was continuing along his route.

Richard ran after the bus. Suddenly, it lurched to the kerb. Passengers spilled out, yelling and coughing. Another bus had pulled up behind it, and after a moment, Richard turned around and climbed on. A few seconds later he got off again and walked back to where Sasha now paced the pavement on bare, charred legs.

He ambled past, snaking his head to stare at Sasha, then turned around and walked past Sasha again, still staring. Then Jamal and

Lloyd got off the 57 and the three of them half walked, half ran to the other bus.

That night, Jasmine noticed that Richard seemed sad.

'What's wrong?' she asked.

He wouldn't tell her.

THE MAN WITH THE MOUSTACHE

After the police arrived, the man with the moustache walked home, tears streaming down his face.

He was in shorts and a button-up shirt, his jacket charred from smothering the flames.

'Why?' he kept asking himself. 'Oh my God, why?'

The school day was long over at five o'clock, but Karl was still in his classroom when Sasha called him on his mobile.

'Dad. I need you to come over here right now. I was on the bus and I got set on fire.'

'What?' Karl said. The reception was terrible. 'Say it again.'

'You have to pick me up and take me to the hospital because someone set me on fire.'

Karl was sure he wasn't hearing right. He walked around his classroom closing windows and gathering his things. 'Wait. Say it again. You were on the bus and *what* happened?'

'I need to go to the hospital. Now.'

And then Karl was running, still on the phone with Sasha, still asking the same question over and over as his feet carried him block after block, down one street and up another until he reached the place where Sasha lay on the pavement in their underwear, shivering and hyperventilating. 'Tell me again. What happened?'

Most of the passengers had dispersed by now, but a few lingered with the driver on the pavement beside the empty bus. One of them, a teenage girl, had called her mother, who had called 911. The girl's mother arrived before the ambulance did. She stood with her arm around her daughter as Karl called Debbie and told her there had been an accident.

When Debbie got there, she thought Sasha must have fallen in mud, because why else would their legs have those black splotches? And then she understood and began to sob.

'Well,' Sasha said. 'It came true. What you were always worried about.'

The ambulance took a long time to arrive. The police, on the other hand, came right away.

'Do you know who did this to you?' the officers kept asking Sasha.

'No.' Sasha's teeth were chattering. 'I was asleep.'

They had never been so cold. Their legs were naked to the November chill. More than naked – skinless, exposed. Karl took off the hat he always wore and used it to shield Sasha's crotch from the eyes of passers-by.

'Don't you have anything to keep him warm?' Debbie asked the cops, forgetting all about Sasha's pronouns. A police officer brought a sheet of yellow plastic from the squad car – the kind usually used for covering corpses. Debbie didn't want to put it over the open wounds on Sasha's legs, so she wrapped it around their shoulders.

135

At last, after maybe forty-five minutes, the ambulance arrived. Paramedics loaded Sasha on to a trolley and hooked up an IV. Warm fluids flowed into Sasha's veins. Morphine. The pain and cold receded. They were safe. Alive. Everything would be OK.

Karl climbed in the front of the ambulance that took Sasha to hospital. There wasn't room for Debbie. She stood on the pavement and wept as they drove away. Everyone had left except the teenage girl and her mother.

'They did it because he was wearing a skirt!' Debbie sobbed.

Together, the girl and her mother wrapped Debbie in their arms. 'That's no reason,' they said.

Sasha was giddy in the emergency room. Talking. Joking. High on morphine. 'It's the Rim Fire's revenge,' they told the doctors, remembering how they had been evacuated from the fire in Yosemite with Nemo. Debbie and Karl had never seen them so social. 'Everybody's so nice,' Sasha gushed. 'They're taking such good care of me!'

Sasha had been taken to Saint Francis Memorial Hospital in San Francisco so that they could be admitted into the Bothin Burn Center, a specialised unit that treats burn victims from around the Bay Area. Dr Richard F. Grossman, one of the burn centre's surgeons, came to the emergency room to assess the situation. The wounds on Sasha's legs were a collage of colours – red, pink, black and yellow – but what Dr Grossman noted immediately was that many of them were white, a leathery colourless char that looked like overcooked tuna. That signaled third-degree burns, in which the skin has burned all the way through, down to the fat below.

From the emergency room, Sasha was taken to the burn unit. The first stop was an enormous stainless-steel tub filled with a solution of diluted bleach. (Infection is one of the leading causes of death for burn victims.) It was there, naked in the tub, that Sasha began to understand the severity of their injuries. Their legs were unrecognisable – weirdly coloured, charred and flaking. Dr Grossman estimated that the burns covered 22 per cent of Sasha's body.

Still, he was reassuring when he met with Debbie and Karl. The burns were very deep, he said, but they were treatable. In the years he'd been at the Bothin Burn Center, he had seen much, much worse. 'We have people die here every few days,' he explained later. 'I knew Sasha would not be one of them.'

THE TEN O'CLOCK NEWS

Every night, Kaprice watched the ten o'clock news. It was part of her preparation for the next day at school. If someone had been shot in Oakland, odds were that somebody at Oakland High School would be connected, affected or implicated.

That night, the news reported that a man had been set on fire on the 57 bus. She shook her head. 'Who would do something like that?' she wondered.

Kaprice got a call from a teacher the next morning, saying one of her children wanted to be excused from class. Then Richard got on the phone. 'I really need to talk to you.'

Kaprice couldn't imagine what was so urgent that it couldn't wait until class was over. 'Come in at lunchtime,' she said.

He was there at lunchtime but her office was filled with kids. She could tell he wanted to talk in private, but clearing the office wasn't easy. One girl didn't want to leave and Kaprice had to physically escort her out of the office, through an antechamber, and into the main hallway. As she did, she heard the door click behind her. She was locked out. Her keys and phone were sitting on her desk.

Annoyed, she walked down the hallway to the main office and threaded her way between desks to the back of the room. There, she dug out the key to a side door that opened into her office. The whole journey couldn't have taken more than a few minutes. But when she stepped back into her office, Richard was gone.

She found him outside, being led away in handcuffs by two uniformed police officers. She never learned what he'd wanted to tell her.

When Sasha didn't show up at school the next day, Nemo was concerned. They asked around – did anyone know where Sasha was? A student who was a neighbour of Sasha's had heard they were in the hospital, but didn't know why.

Nemo called the house. No answer. Then they called Karl's mobile phone, voice shaking. 'Is Sasha okay?'

Debbie and Karl were at the hospital. They told Nemo what had happened – the fire, the burns. The surgeon said the prognosis was good, Karl assured Nemo. Sasha would be OK, but they were going to be in hospital for at least a couple of weeks.

'Tell them I love them,' Nemo said before hanging up.

Nemo told Michael. Michael told Healy. Healy told Teah. The friends huddled together, shaken and in tears. As news spread, life at school came to a halt. It was unfathomable. How could such a thing happen in the queer-friendly Bay Area?

'We were all liberal, hippie teenagers, so we didn't even think of that happening,' Healy says.

But it had. Someone had set Sasha on fire. Inevitably thoughts turned to the person who had done it.

'Hate him,' Healy says. 'Hate his guts.'

Shyam Sundar was the science teacher at Maybeck. A burly, bearded man with a reputation for academic toughness, Shyam taught biology, chemistry and organic chemistry and was somewhat of a legend among the students. There was a card in the index card game titled Shyam. The instructions were, *Imitate Shyam as best you can, child*. Shyam called them all 'child.'

Sasha was his favourite student. 'A scholar,' Shyam called Sasha, the highest compliment he could give. 'Not a scholar-in-training. A scholar.'

On his way to work on 5 November, Shyam heard on the radio that someone had been set on fire on the bus. But it wasn't until Sasha didn't show up at school that he learned what had happened. He doesn't remember exactly how he found out. In fact, he doesn't remember much of anything.

'The whole week is blocked out from my memory,' he says. In his fifteen years of teaching, he had never let anything get in the way of his work. Even when his grandmother died – he got the news in the middle of a lecture and kept right on teaching. 'To me, that's what she would have wanted,' he explains. 'To me, teaching is sacred.'

But after Sasha was burned, he couldn't teach. He still showed up every day, but he just handed out worksheets to his students. Sasha had always sat in the same seat. Now that seat was empty. Shyam found he couldn't even look at that part of the classroom.

'The students who sat there,' he says, 'got no eye contact from me whatsoever.'

Jasmine was watching television when she saw that police had arrested a suspect in the bus passenger burning that had been all over the news. The newsreader didn't say a name, nor did the broadcast show the suspect's face, but Jasmine's heart began pounding all the same. The TV showed the boy's back as he was marched in handcuffs up the steps of the police station. White jeans. Black hoodie. The same clothes Richard had worn to school that morning.

'I knew my baby as soon as I seen him,' she said. 'As soon as I saw his body, I saw his structure, I knew exactly who it was.'

She called Kaprice, who confirmed that Richard had been arrested. Then she began calling everyone she could think of – Richard's father, his probation officer, the police station. No one could tell her where he was. And so she sat and watched the news and waited for someone to contact her. Richard never called. He called his father instead, maybe because he didn't want to face his mother's disappointment. By the time Jasmine was allowed to see him, six days later, the district attorney had decided to charge Richard as an adult and his name was all over the news.

When Richard arrived at the police station on the day of his arrest, the officers placed him in interview room 202 and instructed him to remove his shoelaces, belt, bandanna and the cord from his hoodie. Then they left him there.

The room was small and shabby, containing only a rectangular table and three chairs with blue plastic seats. The plaster was pitted and peeling – pieces littered the floor as if someone had recently punched the wall and no one had bothered sweeping up afterwards. Richard leaned forward and rested his forehead on the edge of the table. Minutes ticked by. He sat up and rubbed his eyes with two fingers. Leaned back in the chair and stared at the floor. Leaned forward with his chin resting on his arms. Cradled his head in his hand. Sat up and rested his chin in his palms. Ten minutes went by. Then twenty. Thirty.

After an hour an officer peeked in to hand him a bag lunch. He unpacked it: a drink, a turkey sandwich, a bag of crisps. He smoothed the paper bag flat and placed the sandwich on top. Then he folded his hands and bowed his head. He crossed himself three times. Then he ate the sandwich.

He had his head down on the table when Officers Anwawn Jones and Jason Anderson came in, two hours and nineteen minutes after he'd first been placed in the room. They moved him into the centre seat and settled themselves on either side of him.

'You didn't eat all your chips, man?' Officer Jones asked. He was tall and African American, with a shaved head, glasses and an easy, sympathetic manner.

'I was getting a little stomachache,' Richard said.

The officers assured him that they wanted to keep things relaxed. They asked about Richard's life – where he lived, what sports he played. 'How are you doing in school?' Officer Jones asked.

'I was doing OK,' Richard admitted. 'But then it started falling off. The school's not good for me. There's too many distractions. I need to go to a smaller environment where I can focus.'

'A lot of kids wouldn't understand that,' Officer Jones said, nodding. 'I had the same issue when I was younger.'

'Any girlfriend right now?' asked Officer Anderson. He was white and heavyset, and though he smiled a lot, his friendliness seemed forced.

'I've been looking,' Richard said.

'Looking?' Anderson grinned. 'On the prowl?'

'It's not looking too good,' Richard said.

'Were there girls up in Redding?' Anderson asked. 'They cool?'

Richard looked puzzled. He'd been in a group home up there, he explained, and hadn't been allowed to mix with girls.

Jones sat with one hand resting on his knee, the other on his writing pad. 'Did you learn something in the group home? Did you learn some important lessons, being away from your family?'

'It was hard,' Richard admitted. 'It took me actually a while. And then I was doing good. And then my best friend since forever, my best friend ever, he passed. And then I had a little breakdown."

'What happened to your friend?' Jones asked.

'He was murdered.'

As the conversation continued, Richard was candid, almost confiding. He told them about getting robbed, about how he'd been set up by someone he'd called a friend. 'I have trust issues right now,' he told the officers.

'Well, here's the deal,' Officer Jones said at last. 'I'm going to explain to you why you're in here. We have some questions we wanted to ask you. So we can get your side of the story, your version of what transpired. But before we get into that, I need to read you your rights.'

'**You have the right to remain silent.** Anything you say can be used against you in a court of law. You have the right to talk to a lawyer and have him present with you while you are being questioned. If you cannot afford a lawyer, one will be appointed to represent you before any questioning. Do you understand the rights I have explained to you?'

'Why did you talk?' Jasmine asked Richard later. 'You should've waited until you talked to either me or your father or a lawyer.'

But studies show that more than 90 per cent of juveniles who are interrogated by police don't wait to talk to a lawyer and don't understand the rights the police have read them. They do what Richard did. They talk.

'Kids are not going to spontaneously ask for a parent,' explains Barry Feld, a law professor at the University of Minnesota and one of the nation's leading experts on juvenile justice. 'They're embarrassed, they're ashamed, they're thinking in their adolescent brains that somehow their parents won't find out. They're thinking, How do I get out of here?'

'They read him his rights, and they asked him, did he understand? He didn't understand,' Jasmine says. 'And I know he didn't understand because *I* could barely understand. When we're in court, I don't know nothing until the lawyer tells me.'

'**You have a pretty good memory**, right?' Officer Jones asked when he finished reading Richard his rights. 'Give me the rundown of what you were doing, say, yesterday, after, say, school. From the time school got out till, say, about eight to nine o'clock at night.' Richard told him about Lloyd meeting him at the gate at the end of the school day and about going with him to get a phone from someone, a process that had taken close to two hours. Then he described getting on the bus and how there was a man on the bus wearing a skirt. He'd just got off the 57 bus to get the express bus, he said, when he heard screams and ran back. When they opened the door to the bus, he saw that the man's skirt was on fire.

'What do you think about dudes who dress up in skirts?' Jones asked.

'I'm not with that,' Richard said. 'I wouldn't say that I hate gay people, but I'm very homophobic.'

Jones nodded. 'OK. Why would you call yourself homophobic?'

'I don't have no problem with somebody if they like men. But like if you do too much? Nobody cares, really.'

'Do too much?'

'Taking it to the next level,' Richard explained.

Jones asked for an example of the next level.

'Cross-dressing and like – some people, like they try to make everybody know that they are that and they try to do too much and – it's just a lot.'

Jones spun his pencil in circles on his notepad, like the spinner for a board game. 'A lot of people share the same views,' he said. 'People who display stuff outwardly for everybody to see.'

Then he asked Richard to go through the events on the bus again.

'I think there's a couple parts where you haven't been completely honest with us,' he said when Richard finished. 'You're a good kid. I like people to be honest with me. We're going to be honest with you. I expect people to be honest with me.'

He asked Richard to describe what he and Lloyd and Jamal had been wearing on the bus the day before. Then he slid some photographs across the table.

Richard. Lloyd. Jamal.

Richard picked them up. Looked them over.

'It's pretty obvious we have some pictures,' Jones said, tucking the pictures under his notebook. 'And mind you, these are not still pictures. These are pictures from video.'

'Both of the buses you were on, they have audio and video cameras,' Anderson added. 'With that in mind, I want you to take a quick second and I want you to rethink the story that you told us. And I want you to tell us what *really* happened.

'You're not a bad kid,' Anderson said. 'Sometimes we make decisions that are not the best decisions. Keeping in mind that you know we have video, and the video shows everything that happened on that bus. Everything. Right now is a time in your life when you've got to decide, am I going to take responsibility for my actions? Am I going to be honest? Because that dude on the bus whose skirt caught on fire got burned pretty good.'

'Can I see the video?' Richard asked.

They only showed him a short snippet of the video, but it was enough. Richard slumped in his chair, one hand shoved in his pocket.

'Why would you set that dress on fire?' Officer Anderson asked.

'Being stupid.' Richard's voice was low.

'What was going through your mind?'

'Nothin'.'

'Have you done this before?'

'No.'

'What would even remotely make you think about setting something on fire like that – someone's clothing?' Anderson persisted. 'That dude got seriously burned. It's not like he went home. He's awaiting surgery at a San Francisco burn centre right now. He got burned real bad. What was going through your mind when you decided to light that dress on fire?'

'Nothing.' It was a whisper now.

'Was it because the dude was wearing a dress? Did you have a problem with him?'

'I don't know.'

'People do things for a reason,' the officer said. 'We've all made decisions in life that may not have been the best choice to make at a given time. What we're trying to figure out is why this happened.'

'I'm homophobic,' Richard said at last. 'I don't like gay people.'

'Really? And you had a problem seeing him on the bus?'

'I don't know what was going through my head,' Richard said. 'I just reacted.'

'Did Jamal or your cousin Lloyd tell you to do it?'

'No.'

'I know you said you didn't know what was going through your mind,' Officer Jones said. 'But did you get angry because he's a gay dude in a skirt, not just being gay but "doing too much"?'

'Actually, I really didn't know that his skirt was going to do that, I didn't know that it was going to catch like that,' Richard blurted. 'It was, like, a little flame. I thought it was just going to go out.'

But it was too late to backpedal. On the charging documents, Officer Jones wrote in block capitals, *DURING SUSP INTERVIEW, THE SUSP STATED HE DID IT BECAUSE HE WAS HOMOPHOBIC.*

A MAN IN A KILT

The news spread quickly, first to local media, then national, then international. 'A man wearing a kilt-like garment was set on fire as he slept on a public bus in Oakland, California, during evening commuter hours,' Reuters news service reported.

'A passenger on an Oakland, Calif., public bus received burns to his legs after his kilt was set on fire,' UPI wrote. The word *kilt* seemed to have got lodged in the minds of reporters. It was in every report, as if Sasha had been on the way home from bagpipe practice. The *Daily Mail* even illustrated the report with a photo of a kilt, explaining that a kilt is 'the national dress of Scotland.'

It felt wrong to Debbie. Sasha wasn't wearing a kilt, they were wearing a *skirt*. And she was pretty certain that the skirt was the reason Sasha had been set on fire. So when a reporter showed up on her doorstep, she began to explain.

'My son considers himself agender,' she said. 'He likes to wear a skirt. It's his statement. That's how he feels comfortable dressing.'

It wasn't until later that she realised she'd gotten the pronouns wrong.

Healy instant-messaged Michael at 9:16 p.m. on Tuesday 5 November.

    Healy: how are you

    Michael: mixed

        and you?

    Healy: [tapping a random assortment of keys]

        fohasjofpivcskm

    Michael: uh huh

    Healy: ya

        you understand

    Michael: it finally kinda hit me in physics class

Healy: It hit me in science but I didn't wanna cry (although i did) but then also when I saw it on the news?

Like this is real this is not fake there are people I've never met who've seen this there are proably people who i've met at cons or talked to on the internet or something who watched and were like thats fucking crazy

Its horrifying

Michael: yeah …

did you hear that sasha's cousin started a fundraiser to help pay for the medical bills?

Healy: Yes, i saw it

it has already raised about 2G

Michael: nice

Healy: i dunno

I guess that they are responding to texts? just an FYI

Michael: they are!?!?!

what makes you think this?

Healy: Yes, they responded to one of Nemos, although they may not be tonite b/c their first surgery is tomorrow

Michael: sasha must be medicated out of their mind …

Healy: You want to know a fun fact?

People's typing generally gets worse if they start crying

Michael: well, I'm glad that they're in contact

I left a message on sasha's phone earlier

Healy: yes, me too!

I did, and I sent them a REALLLLLLLLY long text

Michael: aw

now I feel like I should do something else

Healy: yes well I am a worry-type person

Wait that shouldn't make you feel bad

don't feel bad

Michael: so, I was going to start on the bio essays tonight

Healy: ME TOO

but I haven't

Michael: but there's no way I'll be able to focus

Healy: yeah …

I got basically nothing done tonight

Michael: I want to ask shyam for an extension, but I feel like that would be profiteering off of sasha's injury …

Healy: yes, I thought of that, but it seems unfair and I refuse to.

I'd rather just stay up late well, not rather persay it just seems a better option\more moral option?

something like that

… Are you really okay I don't think your okay as you want everyone to think

Michael: I'm not sure what I feel like

my emotions are changing wildly minute to minute

Healy: Yeah, I dunno, i just feel kinda … numb, now

Michael: one second I'm getting ready to bawl my eyes out, the next I'm somber

I don't want to do anything right now

homework?no

cookie clicker?no

I want to share a link to a news article about sasha, but I'm not sure what I'd write and I kinda just don't want to talk about it on facebook

Healy: yeah, everything just feels, wrong

did you watch the video i sent

I thought it was okay

you?

Michael: yeah

that guy at the end was kinda odd

'I think it might have been due to video games'

that guy was weird …

Healy: yeah, he was

I don't like him

We 'Don't know for sure' but I'm pretty sure it
was a hate crime, IDK about you weirdo

Michael: yeah

there's pretty much no way that it wasn't

Healy: Uh-huh

I must go

enjoy your night

Michael: yeah, right

sleep well

BOOKED IN

The police car pulls up by the side of Alameda County Juvenile Hall and the officers escort you into the booking room. A sign on the wall says:

**ALL PERSONAL
PROPERTY
REMOVED IN THIS
AREA INCLUDING
PIERCINGS WIGS
AND DETACHABLE
HAIR PIECES**

The police have already taken your personal belongings and put them in a bag with your name on it. Now a Juvenile Hall employee asks the police officer to remove your handcuffs.

'Take off your shoes,' the employee instructs. He pats you down and has you walk through the ViewScan metal detector, which will locate any hidden weapons. Another sign explains:

NOTICE:
WE DO NOT RETURN
CIGARETTES
LIGHTERS/MATCHES
TOOLS, KNIVES, DRUGS,
GANG-RELATED PARAPHENALIA OR
ANY ITEM DEEMED
INAPPROPRIATE FOR
MINORS.

They take your clothes and hand you the replacements: khaki trousers, green undershirt, charcoal-gray sweatshirt. Underclothes: white bra and pants for the girls, white boxers for the boys, white socks for everyone. Boxy black shoes, plus slides for the shower. You can take a shower now if you want. Most people do. Chances are, you've been sweating.

When you're dressed, you'll go into the holding tank. There are five of them – concrete-slab boxes with the walls painted white. Nothing in there but a stainless-steel sink and toilet and a call box so you can communicate with the staff. You might be alone in there, or, if it's a busy day, you might be with someone else. They check to make sure they don't put two kids together who have a preexisting beef – they don't want fights.

Once they locate your paperwork, they'll start booking you in. You get two phone calls. One to a parent or guardian, the other to your employer if you have a job, or your probation officer if you're on probation. Then you get a medical screening: 'Are you on medication?' 'Any injuries in the last twenty-four hours?' They'll offer you an HIV test and, if you're a girl, a pregnancy test. If you've been here before, you already have a medical file. They'll thumb through it, checking up. 'How's your asthma?' they might ask.

Then it's time for photographs and fingerprinting. They document your scars and tattoos. Put your prints in the database. And then you're done. Booked in. The whole thing takes less than an hour.

Down a long hallway with mustard-coloured walls. The floor is linoleum, shiny clean, patterned in squares of tan, yellow and beige. Younger kids charged with serious crimes go into unit 4, one of two maximum-security units. Each unit has thirty single rooms spread over two tiers, one upper, one lower. These days the units are only half full.

The doors are blue, the stairs are blue. The rooms are yellow and bare of anything except a single blue bunk, a steel sink and toilet, and a call box by the door. Eight feet by eight feet and brightly lit. A steel door with a square of window. If you're like most kids, once the door slams behind you you'll stand at that window looking out.

There's not much else to look at, unless you count your blurred reflection in the metal mirror over the sink. Nothing to do but look at the sliver of the world you can see through that square of glass or lie down on the blue vinyl-covered mattress, shut your eyes, try to get your heart to stop banging against the wall of your chest.

You won't be leaving the unit anytime soon, except for court appearances, and the weekend visiting hours – three hours on Saturday or Sunday, parents or guardians only, no siblings. Aside from PE, which takes place in the gym down the hall, and a visit to the medical unit, everything you do you'll do here, in this unit, with these same people. School is here. Meals are here. Chapel's here. A barber comes in twice a week to give haircuts in the chair in the corner. The nurse comes here. The counsellor too. The rec yard is just outside the door.

There's another rec yard, big and open, three basketball hoops. It's surrounded by razor wire, but also by hills and trees and sky, a three-hundred-and-sixty-degree view of the world, *the world*. But if you've been charged as an adult, you can't go out there. Your exercise will take place on the triangular yard outside the unit – thirty yards by twenty yards by twenty yards, with a mural of wildlife hung above the basketball backstop. Tilt your head back and you see a pie-shaped wedge of sky through a screen of wire mesh.

After they book you in for something serious – murder, attempted murder, setting a person on fire on a bus – they put you in a camera room for the first twenty-four hours. They know that as soon as you're alone, it's going to hit you. What you did. What could happen. So they watch to make sure you don't become your own next victim.

SURGERY

The first morning in hospital, Sasha was overcome by anxiety. They didn't want to eat, couldn't keep anything down. It's a common reaction to losing your skin: cold, clammy fear. That's why sedatives and antianxiety medicines are as much a part of burn treatment as painkillers.

Sasha needed to eat – burn victims require extra nutrition to heal, and Sasha wasn't a big eater to begin with. The hospital nutritionist wanted to give them a nutritional supplement through a feeding tube that would be inserted through their nose. Sasha objected at first because the supplement wasn't vegan, but Debbie and Karl persuaded them to set aside their principles just this once. 'This is going to get you out of here sooner,' they promised.

The next morning, 6 November, Sasha went into surgery. In the operating room, Dr Grossman shaved away at the burned, dead skin, cutting away thin layers until he reached bleeding tissue. Then he covered the open wound with a temporary graft of pig skin. This xenograft, as it's called, would stay in place until the underlying tissue had regenerated enough to supply blood to the skin graft.

By now, Sasha's name was on the news. As Debbie and Karl stood at the nurses' station talking with the burn unit's director, a call came from the lobby. Someone was there to visit Sasha. He said his name was Max and he claimed to be 'a pastor from Sasha's hometown.' After that, Debbie and Karl drew up a short list of approved visitors along with a plan for dealing with the press.

That evening, Sasha checked out the news coverage online, but the spectacle didn't hold their interest. Their mind drifted, dulled by painkillers and sedatives. News from the outside world was like listening to the radio on a drive through the mountains – the distant voices clear for a moment, then warbling, and then washing into static.

Debbie and Karl didn't talk to Sasha about it, but Debbie had spoken to one of the police officers who had interviewed Richard. She took notes on what he told her about Richard:

He actually said he's homophobic. He giggled.

Michael messaged Healy at 7:02 p.m. on Wednesday 6 November.

Michael: hey, you there?

Healy: yush< je suis

Michael: how're you?

Healy: [tapping a random assortment of keys] uhfwcanovdwbjhgwoeaihs

I got to text sasha while I was babysitting

That was nice

Michael: nice

yeah, I caught them on skype earlier

hey, gmail says they're online

glad to see they're awake

Healy: yes, I was JUST texting them, like, 20 mins ago

Michael: indeed

Nemo and I are visiting him tomorrow

*them

Healy: Oh, thats nice

i wish I could

didn't know they were allowed visitors

well, maybe I'll go on Friday (?)

I can bring them a pic of sasha skirt day~

Michael: sasha skirt day?

Healy: didn't you hear? we're all wearing skirts on Friday for sasha and were gonna take a pic~

Michael: no one told me this

I approve

Healy: I'M GOING TO WEAR A SKIRT

Its a big deal

I hate skirts

Michael: heh

does sasha know of this yet?

Healy: nooooooo its a surprise no telling

Michael: this is gonna be fun

Healy: yes tis

how are YOU feeling?

Michael: a lot better

taking a day off was a good idea

Healy: thats good

getting to talk to them helped me, but I'm still kinda dying

Now I feel like shit, AND I'm not done with my HW

Michael: yeah … I didn't get much work done today, either

I have a late night ahead of me …

Healy: I can't sleep

Everytime I close my eyes, i freak out

I didn't sleep except for maybe an hour or 2 last night

Michael: :(

I was exausted, personally

I fell asleep as soon as my head hit the pillow

Healy: yeah, but I was just, I mean, think about it, they woke up and they were on fire

CHARGES

Two days after Richard's arrest, the district attorney's office released his name to the media. He was being charged as an adult, which meant he no longer had the protections given to juveniles, one of which is anonymity. They charged him with two felonies: 'aggravated mayhem' and 'assault with intent to cause great bodily injury.' Each charge also contained a hate-crime clause that would increase Richard's sentence by an additional one to three years in state prison. If convicted, he faced a maximum sentence of life in prison, a punishment he would never have faced if he had been charged as a juvenile.

'[Richard ——'s] violent and senseless criminal conduct resulted in severe and traumatic injuries to a young and entirely innocent victim,' Alameda County district attorney Nancy O'Malley said. 'The intentional and callous nature of the crime is shocking and will not be tolerated in our community.'

Lloyd and Jamal were never interviewed, arrested or charged.

'Stop right here, and for a moment imagine yourself forced to submit to being handcuffed, and see what kind of feelings will be aroused in you,' a Chicago lawyer named John P. Altgeld wrote in an 1884 book called *Our Penal Machinery and Its Victims*. Arguing that 'submission to that one act of degradation prepares many a young man for a career of crime,' he took the reader through the experience of a youthful offender – which began with the accused, usually arrested for vagrancy or disorderly conduct, spending the night in the police station among older, more vicious criminals. He compared the criminal justice system to 'a great mill which, somehow or other, supplies its own grist, a maelstrom which draws from the outside, and then keeps its victims moving in a circle until swallowed in the vortex.'

Altgeld was part of a movement headed by two prominent reformers, Lucy Flower and Julia Lathrop, whose work led to the establishment of the nation's first juvenile court, in Cook County,

Illinois, in 1899. Young offenders, these reformers argued, were different from adults. They were works in progress, malleable, and could be set on the right path if the law behaved like a stern but loving parent rather than as an instrument of punishment.

The notion that juvenile offenders are fundamentally different from adult ones lasted for more than eighty years. Then came the crime wave of the late 1980s and early 1990s. As crack and guns flooded the cities and gangs battled over turf, the violent-crime rate for juveniles aged fifteen to seventeen doubled, as did the violent-crime rate for people aged eighteen to twenty. John J. Dilulio Jr, a political scientist at Princeton University, argued that we were seeing a new kind of juvenile criminal, utterly unlike the misbehaving teens of the past. He called them 'super-predators.'

'A super-predator is a young juvenile criminal who is so impulsive, so remorseless, that he can kill, rape, maim without giving it a second thought,' he explained. And he warned that the numbers of these 'fatherless, Godless, and jobless' teens were growing. By the mid-2000s, he predicted, their numbers would double or even triple, unleashing a tidal wave of violence across the nation. 'As many as half of these juvenile super-predators could be young black males,' Dilulio wrote in a 1996 article entitled 'My Black Crime Problem, and Ours.'

In response, one state after another enacted 'direct-file' laws, which allowed juvenile offenders to be transferred to adult courts if they committed certain crimes. 'There are no violent offences that are juvenile,' thundered Newt Gingrich, who was then Speaker of the US House of Representatives. 'You rape somebody, you're an adult. You shoot somebody, you're an adult.'

California's direct-file law, Proposition 21, was approved by 62 per cent of the voters in March 2000. Billed as a way to get tough on gang violence and drive-by shootings, the measure increased the sentences for a number of different crimes, and it gave prosecutors the power to decide on their own if they wanted to file charges in adult court against offenders as young as fourteen. Previously, prosecutors wanting to charge a juvenile as an adult had to make their case in a hearing before a juvenile-court judge. Prop 21 allowed them to make the call on their own in certain cases, and made the call for them in others. Some crimes, mostly sex crimes, now *had* to be prosecuted in adult court.

Nine months after the passage of Proposition 21, 30 per cent of all teen offenders in California were being charged as adults. In some areas of the state, the percentage was much higher – in San Diego County, for example, three out of every four young people were charged as adults by the end of that first year.

This wasn't because more juveniles were committing crimes. Juvenile arrest rates began to fall in 1994, and they have continued to fall ever since. Today, the FBI's juvenile violent-crime index, which measures arrests for murder, rape, robbery and aggravated assault, is lower than it was in 1980, and that's true across racial lines. The violent-crime rate among black youths, in fact, has dropped by 60 per cent in the past two decades, and the homicide rate has dropped by 82 per cent.

The super-predator apocalypse was a myth.

Yet many of the laws that the scare put on the books are still used. While California voters effectively repealed Proposition 21 in 2016, many states continue to routinely treat juveniles as adults.

Each year, an estimated 250,000 US juveniles are transferred into adult courts. In California, three-quarters of those juveniles are transferred by prosecutors using the discretion given to them by Proposition 21. This discretion has not been evenly applied. A 2012 analysis by California's Department of Justice found that cases against black youths were more than twice as likely to be directly filed in adult court than cases against white youths, and cases against Latino youths were more than six times as likely. And the disparity didn't end there. Once they landed in adult court, young black and brown offenders were also much more likely to serve time. Just one-third of white youths were sentenced to adult or juvenile state correctional facilities in 2012, while two-thirds received more lenient treatment and were given probation, or sentenced to serve time in county jails. For kids of colour, the ratios were reversed – two-thirds served time in state facilities, while only one-third received probation or jail. Nationally, 58 per cent of all incarcerated African American youths are serving their time in adult prisons.

'What he did was a terrible thing,' Jasmine said after Richard was charged. 'I'm not trying to defend his actions because it was very terrible.' Even so, she said, Richard was a kid, a kid who was capable of making an exceedingly dumb mistake, but one who was also capable of learning from it.

'Life in jail? A sixteen-year-old? It's ridiculous,' she said. 'They need to give him time to grow. Why lock him up and have him institutionalised and make him worse?'

COURT DATE

On 7 November, the day Richard made his first court appearance, reporters packed the hallways.

'What kind of boy is he?' one shouted as Jasmine and her sister Juliette stepped into the lift with Richard's grandmother.

'He's a good kid. A *very* good kid,' the grandmother, also named Juliette, said.

'Why do you think he did this?' another reporter asked.

'I don't know. He was with his friends, joking around, that's all,' she said.

'He's not a bad person. If you knew him you'd know he's always joking around,' Richard's aunt Juliette said in a separate interview. 'He shouldn't have did what he did. I feel so bad.'

Jasmine spoke to the press too, off camera. 'I am very sorry for my son's actions,' she said. 'I did not raise my son that way.'

That's what they said.

But all anyone seemed to hear was this: 'He was joking around.' 'Setting someone on fire because of their clothes is not a joke or prank gone awry,' editorialised the *Bay Area Reporter*, a newspaper serving the LGBTQ community. 'As Alameda County prosecutors correctly see it, it's a felony, and [Richard] surely isn't laughing at the possibility of life in prison because he apparently couldn't handle someone dressing differently.'

Online forums seethed with outrage.

To the Mother of the 16 year old who set the fire. You call that just joking around? Suppose some kid set you on fire, burned say 90% of your body. Would that be joking around? Your son needs life in prison! For attempted murder! a man named Brian Weil wrote on an anti-bullying Facebook page. The comment received 160 'likes'.

On news sites, blogs and forums around the country, the conclusion was the same: Lock him up. Throw away the key. Lock up the mother too while you're at it.

Many suggested far worse.

REELING

Jasmine felt the world had spun off its axis.

It was impossible, and yet it was true.

Richard had hurt someone, really hurt them. Somebody who hadn't done anything to anyone.

She was mad at Richard. She was mad at Lloyd. She was mad at herself. She was mad at society. How could this have happened?

She knew what people were saying about Richard, about her. She'd seen the online comments. Her sister Juliette advised her not to tell anyone about Richard's arrest, but she wasn't going to hide. 'If you have anything to say, bad comments, take it to God,' she told everyone who asked about Richard. 'Pray for him.'

THE DESK

Nancy O'Malley, the Alameda County district attorney, worked at a weighty dark-wood desk that was once used by Earl Warren, the US Supreme Court justice whose court ruled that public school segregation was against the US Constitution in the landmark 1954 decision *Brown vs. Board of Education.* A round-faced blonde with a brisk, no-nonsense manner, she was known as a crusader for the rights of women and children – her prosecutorial priorities included sex trafficking, domestic violence and child abuse. She had a reputation as tough, but generally fair. Her office had one of the lowest direct-file rates in the state. But in this particular case, O'Malley had no qualms about prosecuting Richard as an adult.

'The crime is very, very, very serious,' she explained. 'But for some Good Samaritans, Sasha could very well be dead. He lit

Sasha's skirt on fire on the bus in the middle of the day and that's very, very disturbing behaviour. If the defendant doesn't change and get rehabilitated, he's a very serious person in our society and a real threat to anyone.'

A threat, she argued, because hate crimes are discrimination, just as segregation was. And as the occupant of Earl Warren's desk, she was determined to fight discrimination wherever she found it.

'We have a history, a long history in this country, of people and cultures who have been treated badly because of their race, their gender, their religion, and all the protected classes that we've identified under the law,' she explained. 'So if somebody commits a heinous crime against somebody because they are a member of a protected class, that is very purposeful discrimination. It's important to show that this is the kind of behaviour that will never be tolerated.'

Until the mid-1980s, the law made no distinction between crimes motivated by bigotry and crimes motivated by money, passion, or boredom. Murder was murder; vandalism was vandalism. The term *hate crime* was coined in response to what was described at the time as an 'epidemic' of neo-Nazi and skinhead violence, although in retrospect it's unclear whether any such epidemic existed. Since then, the number of bias-motivated prosecutions has steadily gone down. In California, a state with close to 39 million people, hate-crime prosecutions have fallen 48 per cent since 2003, with just 158 bias crimes filed for prosecution in 2012. (Since bias crimes are vastly underreported, however, the true number is undoubtedly higher than the statistics indicate.)

But despite how infrequently they're prosecuted, high-profile hate crimes offer a powerful narrative, one that has been important in fighting prejudice. A hate crime is bias boiled down to its most vile essence. Even someone who isn't sure what they think about *hiring* people who are black, gay or transgender can feel the essential wrongness of *hurting* someone because they are black, gay or transgender. By revealing the raw ugliness at the heart of prejudice, high-profile hate-crime prosecutions have helped to build empathy for people on the margins. Perhaps the most high-profile hate-crime prosecutions in Alameda County history were against four men who murdered a transgender teenager named Gwen Araujo in 2002, after discovering her biological sex. In the wake of that case, California's state legislature passed the Gwen Araujo Justice for Victims Act, which allows juries to be instructed before they begin deliberations that they should not allow themselves to be influenced by bias against the gender identity of the victim, defendant or witnesses.

Yet the majority of hate-crime offenders don't fit the stereotype of the squinting, bristle-headed loner with a swastika tattoo. Researchers estimate that fewer than 5 per cent are members of an organised hate group. Most are young males, either in their teens or early twenties, acting in a group, often immediately after school. In a study of Boston hate-crime prosecutions in the early 1990s, two-thirds of the offenders were categorised as 'thrill-seeking' – that is, they were groups of young people 'looking for some fun' at the expense of someone they regarded as lower status. The authors of the study found that many of these offenders weren't even particularly biased toward their victims, but were following the lead of a more biased peer.

Many hate crimes, according to Phyllis B. Gerstenfeld, a criminal-justice professor at California State University, Stanislaus, 'don't have as much to do with the victim as they do with the offender and their own insecurity – which of course is a lot of what's going on with adolescents in general.'

Maybe that's why Nancy O'Malley received a surprising letter in November 2013. The letter was from two groups that might have been expected to support O'Malley's decision to charge Richard as an adult: the National Center for Lesbian Rights and the Transgender Law Center.

'When juvenile impulsivity and poor judgment produce dire consequences, it does not make sense to craft a response intended for adults,' they said in a letter that was also sent on behalf of the American Civil Liberties Union of Northern California. 'Rather, these are the very circumstances under which it is important to remember that children are different from adults.'

The letter concluded: 'We firmly believe that you can demonstrate your office's commitment to protecting the victims of hate crimes without imposing adult sanctions on juvenile offenders.'

When people say 'Children are different from adults,' what do they mean? Is a sixteen-year-old really a child? By that age, surely any rational person knows not to go around setting people's clothing on fire. That, anyway, was the argument made by many online commenters:

He's 16 not 10. If he doesn't know by now that trying to kill other people is bad, then its a bit too late for him. Some people can not be fixed, if he behave like an animal then he should be treated like one, one wrote.

If you have to be "taught why" and you're 16, then you're never going to be anything but a threat or a curse to everyone around you, wrote another.

It's true that in terms of pure intellect, teenagers are just as smart as adults, just as able to reason, and just as knowledgeable about the consequences of risky behaviour. But they are also wired differently. Many people have observed that adolescents tend to be more reckless, impulsive and vulnerable to peer pressure than adults. It turns out that at least part of the explanation for this behaviour can be found in the structure of the teenage brain.

The limbic system is the part of the brain that detects things in the environment that we should pay attention to and sends an emotional signal about what to do in response: *Avoid! Investigate! Eat! Fight! Flirt!* Starting around puberty, the limbic system becomes more sensitive to stimulus, which is one reason teenagers become both more emotional and more interested in having new and intense experiences.

Throughout adolescence, the brain is busily lining important neural pathways with a fatty sheath called myelin. Myelin is often likened to the plastic coating around electrical wires – it insulates the neural circuits, making them about a hundred times faster than unmyelinated circuits.

The very last part of the brain to get myelinated is the prefrontal cortex – the part of the brain responsible for reason, planning and deliberation. So while teenage emotions have gone into hyperdrive, reason and logic are still obeying the speed limit.

The result is that while teenagers can make decisions that are just as mature, reasoned and rational as adults' decisions in normal circumstances, their judgement can be fairly awful when they are feeling intense emotions or stress, conditions that psychologists call *hot cognition*. In those situations, teens are more likely to make decisions with the limbic system rather than the prefrontal cortex. The presence of peers is one of the things that raises the emotional stakes, making it more likely that teens will seek out risk and short-term reward without pausing to consider the consequences.

'Even the brightest, best-meaning teenager doesn't tend to think much beyond the moment, especially when they're with their friends,' observes Gerstenfeld.

As people grow up, they generally get better at making thoughtful decisions even when under pressure. Studies have found that around the world, antisocial behaviour increases by a factor of ten during adolescence and then begins to taper off as people reach their early twenties (criminologists call this the *age-crime curve*).

But it doesn't always. Some people start committing crimes when they're young and keep on committing them, progressing from burglary to robbery to murder. The problem is, there's no way to know which kid is going to mellow with age and which one is just getting warmed up. 'You cannot tell when you're looking at a sixteen-year-old whether they are irredeemably depraved,' explains Barry Feld, a law professor at the University of Minnesota who is one of the foremost experts on juvenile justice in the US.

So how should we look at teenagers who commit bias crimes? Are they kids with deep-seated character flaws who are likely to be antisocial bigots for the rest of their lives? Or are they simply manifesting the worst aspects of adolescence – an obsession with conformity, group identity and peer approval combined with an appetite for risk and sensation?

Or are they at a fork in the road, a place where their future will be determined by what happens next?

'The proponents of hate-crime laws are liberals, and yet they are the ones who are the biggest critics of mass incarceration,' observes James B. Jacobs, director of New York University's Center for Research in Crime and Justice, and an expert on hate-crime laws. 'So there are ironies piled on ironies. The remedy here is imprisonment, and prisons are the ultimate incubators of antisocial attitudes.'

The first surgery was soon followed by a second.
Dr Grossman needed to cut away more dead tissue – he felt that
the wounds still weren't clean enough for a skin graft. After that,
things settled into a routine. By the end of the first week of Sasha's
hospitalisation, Debbie and Karl had returned to work part-time,
arriving at the hospital every afternoon around two p.m. and staying
into the evening.

Sasha didn't have the concentration to read or watch movies, so
they spent their time dozing, scrolling idly through Tumblr, and
calculating how long it would be until they got another dose of
painkillers. *What makes you get out of bed in the morning?* a
friend asked Sasha on Tumblr as part of a list of get-to-know-you
questions that got passed from person to person.

it used to be not wanting to miss the bus and be late to school,
Sasha wrote. *now it's my nurses taking me to the tub*

Being bathed in the huge stainless-steel tub was Sasha's favourite part of the day. The official name for it was hydrotherapy – the purpose was to keep the wounds clean and prevent infection. All Sasha knew was that the water and towels were warm. It was pleasant, floating there, a welcome change from lying in bed waiting for the next dose of Dilaudid.

Friends came to visit, dressed in yellow paper gowns, their hands covered by blue synthetic-rubber gloves and their faces hidden behind paper masks. Two visitors were allowed in at a time. Nemo and Michael were the first to come. Healy visited a few days later, with Teah. Sasha had asked them not to bring food because everyone had been bringing food. They brought food anyway – vegan sushi from Berkeley.

It was nice to have visitors, but Sasha wanted to go home. It was hard to sleep at the hospital. The room was always too hot or too cold, and it was often permeated with odd noises. For a while, Sasha's roommate was a man in a medically-induced coma who was hooked up to a breathing machine that hissed and thumped in a rhythmic pattern. Their next roommate had burns over half his body – he'd gotten them in a house fire after running back to save his dog. He was friendly and chatty at first – more chatty than Sasha was in the mood for, actually. Then his burns became infected and he grew quieter. At night he moaned and murmured in his sleep.

Andrew didn't visit. He planned to. But when the day arrived there was always a reason not to go. 'I could have done it if I just set aside my bullshit feelings and been there for them,' he said.

The 'bullshit feelings' had to do with a worry that he hadn't been as good a friend to Sasha as Sasha had been to him. That year he'd had his first real boyfriend. The relationship was all-consuming in a not entirely healthy way and Sasha had felt like a third wheel whenever they were together. And of course Andrew and Sasha went to different schools and had different friends, and it was totally normal to grow apart. Except that Sasha had once been the most important person in the world to Andrew and he felt bad and weird about the fact that they weren't close anymore. Like maybe it was his fault. And then he felt bad and weird about feeling bad and weird. So maybe it would be uncomfortable if he showed up at the hospital.

But then Andrew would remember how Sasha had visited him when he was hospitalised for depression two years before. Sasha had come to the hospital on Andrew's fifteenth birthday and they had brought a present, a gift card for an art supply store. It had been so good to see Sasha's face that day. Sasha had been so upbeat. Not in a cheery, let's-put-a-good-face-on-this way, but in a God-I'm-so-happy-you're-OK way.

Now that the situation was reversed, the least he could do was return the favour. Just *show up*, for Christ's sake. He should go. He *would* go. He'd visit Sasha tomorrow. Next week at the latest.

But he never did.

'I had no idea how to even go in the room,' he said later. Because Sasha would be there, in a hospital bed, burned. And the thought of seeing that, of seeing what could happen to gender-nonconforming people, made Andrew's palms grow slick with fear.

'I knew I wasn't in danger by being there – that's silly,' he said. 'But it was just like, "This is how it is for people like us. This is the reality."'

8 November 2013

Dear Victum,

I apologize for my actions, for the pain that I brought to you & your family. I was wrong for what I did. I was wrong. I had no reason to do that to you I don't know what was going through my head at that time. Im not a monster, I have a big heart I never even thought of hurting anyone like the way I hurt you. I just wanted you to know that im deeply sorry for my actions I think about what happened every second, I pray that you heal correctly & that you recover and live a happy life. Please forgive me that's all I want. I take responsibility for all my actions, Ill take all the consequences. I wish you and your family the best of luck. I'm not just saying this because im incarcerated I honestly mean every word.

Love,

Richard —

INTO THE BRIEFCASE

Within days of his arrest, Richard's family scraped the money together to hire a lawyer to handle his defence. They chose Bill Du Bois, a courtly forty-year veteran of the Alameda County Courthouse who had represented a number of high-profile defendants, including one of the men who murdered the transgender teenager Gwen Araujo in 2002.

At their first meeting, Richard gave Du Bois two letters he'd handwritten to Sasha, the one he wrote on 8 November and a second he wrote on 11 November. Du Bois took the letters and tucked them away in his briefcase. Because the letters contained an admission of guilt, he felt he couldn't send them until the case was resolved.

It would be fourteen months before Sasha read them.

SKIRTS FOR SASHA

On Friday 8 November, everyone at Maybeck wore a skirt. Teachers, students, staff. Even Healy, who didn't own any skirts. She used a pinafore that she'd worn as a costume in a play. Ian dressed as much like Sasha as he could manage, in a skirt, kneesocks, flat cap and vest. Nemo wore a tartan skirt over jeans. Michael wore a black miniskirt along with his signature khaki jacket and gray beanie. A photo of Maybeck students holding a sign saying SKIRTS FOR SASHA was taken by a photographer for the San Jose *Mercury News* and reposted to dozens of LGBTQ and anti-bullying blogs.

A week later, under the light of a three-quarter moon, roughly 150 supporters, including students from both Maybeck and Oakland High Schools, marched along the route of the 57 bus.

The march started at the street corner where Richard and Lloyd had got on the bus the week before. Television cameras jockeyed for position, nearly knocking each other over in their eagerness to get the best shot. The kids from Maybeck peered curiously at Oakland High School. Most of them had never seen it before.

'For a minute there was a lot of anger toward Oakland High School at Maybeck,' Michael recalls. 'But they were really good at distancing themselves from the guy who lit Sasha on fire.'

Drums beat in the background, keeping time with the thwup-thwup-thwup of the news helicopters overhead as the marchers tied rainbow ribbons to the bus stop poles between O High and the spot where Sasha usually got off. People carried balloons and glow sticks and signs that said ACCEPT EVERYONE and WE'RE ALL SASHA.

GET WELL! the signs said. WE HECKA LOVE YOU, SASHA!

11 November 2013

Dear Mr ——,

Its me again Richard ——. I just wanted to say that Im
still very sorry and I hope your getting better. I had a
nightmare last night and I woke up sweating and
apologizing. I really hope you get back to the way you
were. I went to court yesterday and there still making me
seem like a monster, but I'm not. I'm a good kid if you get
to know me. Im sure you would have been a nice person
to. I regret what I did, I didn't know that your clothing
would catch like it did, even though I had no reson to do
it anyways. I don't know what was going through my
head. I've commited a stupid act of violence and im going

to be punished for that, and I accept all consequences that I receive because you didn't deserve this I didn't even know you and I still don't. I was hoping that I can meet you face to face so I can apologize to you. I am being charged with great bodily injury and a hate crime. I accept the first charge but the hate crime is wrong. I don't have a problem with homosexual's I have friends that's homosexuals and we never had problems so I don't look at you wrong because of your sexualitie. Honestly I could care less if you like men you wasn't trying to talk to me in that way. I just hope that you forgive me for the pain I brought you and your family.

I am not a thug, gangster, hoodlum, nor monster. Im a young African American male who's made a terrible mistake. Not only did I hurt you but I hurt your family & friends and also my family & friends for I have brought shame to them and our country and I shall be punished which is going to be hard for me because I'm not made to be incarcerated.

In the Bible (Jeremiah 1:5) it says "Before I formed you in the womb I knew you, and before you were born I consecrated you: I appointed you a prophet to the nations."

Consecrated means to dedicate somebody or something to a particular purpose. I'm not saying im a prophet. What im saying is God knew us before we were anything and he made a plan for us all, and we know its not evil because God isn't evil so we wasn't made to do bad things. I really don't know why I did what I did but I hope you dont think im evil im actually good. I've also been hurt alot for no reason, not like I hurt you but Ive been hurt physically and mentally so I know how it feels, the pain and confusion of why me I've felt it before plenty of times so I know how it feels. So get better and Im looking forward to meeting you so I can apoligize, im going to write you at least two letters a week so be expecting them. Also I'll keep you in my prayers.

Get well

Signed,
Richard —

Richard didn't end up writing more letters. But on 11 November, Karl wrote a letter of his own. It was sent to the parents and staff at Sequoia Elementary School, where he taught kindergarten.

I think it's really important to keep in mind that none of us can know the mind, motivations, or intentions of the person who set flame to Sasha's clothing, he wrote.

Oakland Police have a 16-year-old high school student in custody, based on video camera footage from the bus. As far as I know, police are the only people who have viewed the footage. I certainly haven't, so I can only guess at what happened. At this point, I choose to assume that this kid was playing with fire, and that he gravely underestimated the consequences of that. Others may make different assumptions, but it's important to remember that they are all just that: assumptions. So when I talk to my students about this, I will emphasize the importance of fire safety. "Don't play with matches or lighters." And of course "Stop, Drop, and Roll" if your clothing catches fire.

He also offered language for explaining Sasha's gender identity:

Being agender simply means that the person doesn't feel they are "either a boy or a girl." I realize this is a concept that even adults have difficulty wrapping their heads around. (My wife and I frequently slip up in our pronoun usage, much to Sasha's chagrin!) So I can't pretend that it's an issue that all young children will grasp. But what they certainly can and should understand is that different people like different things. Different people dress or behave or look differently. And that's a GOOD thing. Sasha feels comfortable wearing a skirt. It's part of their style. They also frequently sport a necktie and vest. Sasha likes the look, and frankly, so do I. It makes me smile to see Sasha being Sasha.

As I wrote above, none of us can know the mind of the kid who lit a flame to Sasha's skirt. But I have a feeling that if he had seen Sasha's skirt as an expression of another kid's unique, beautiful self, and had smiled and thought, "I hella love Oakland," I wouldn't be writing this now.

Again, many thanks for all of your love and kindness. Let's all take care of each other.

—Karl —

Richard's extended family showed up for his second court appearance, on 15 November, including Jasmine's cousin Regis, who is gay. Tall, attractive and androgynous, Regis didn't talk to the press. But his presence was a statement in itself – I'm here, I'm queer and I support my cousin.

Inside the courtroom, reporters discussed the best terms to use when describing Sasha. Gender fluid? Genderqueer? Gender nonconforming? Agender?

'I just say he was wearing a skirt,' one reporter offered. He gave a weary shrug. 'The terms change all the time.'

Nothing much happened in court, other than Du Bois announcing his plans to file a motion contesting the decision to try Richard as an adult. Afterward, he took questions from reporters.

'I've met the minor and I can tell you he's not homophobic, not even remotely,' he said. 'First of all, he doesn't know how to spell homophobic, much less be it.'

Everyone had their own theory as to why Richard had used the term. Du Bois said when he asked Richard for a definition, Richard had said that it meant he wasn't gay, that he liked girls. Jasmine said that she thought he was trying to get out of trouble by saying what he thought the police wanted him to say. But whatever his reason for saying it, it was part of the story now. Newsreaders mentioned it almost every time they reported a new development.

'This is not a whodunit,' Du Bois said. 'This is not even a "what happened?" This is what frame of mind the kid had.'

The attorney tended to talk about the case with a mixture of calm and exasperation, as if his powers of incredulity had already been strained to the point of breaking. He argued that the views Richard expressed in the police interview were nothing more sinister than a kid being weirded out by the sight of a boy in a skirt.

'They're putting him in the category of skinhead because he admitted to being homophobic. To being "very homophobic." And they're saying, "We take that as true."' He bugged out his eyes and dropped his jaw to indicate how absurd this was.

'Lynchings – *they're* hate crimes,' he said. 'But the kid who thinks that [wearing a skirt] is anomalous and decides to play a prank is not committing a hate crime.'

On Sasha's first full day in hospital, a stranger dropped off a bouquet of silk flowers – three white roses and four stalks of orange Chinese lanterns. A former burn victim herself, she knew that real flowers aren't allowed in the burn ward because of the risk of infection.

That was the beginning. Within days, letters and packages began arriving at the hospital, at Maybeck High School, at Debbie and Karl's home. An online medical fund set up by Sasha's cousin raised more than $31,000 in donations.

'What did I get today?' Sasha asked each afternoon when Debbie and Karl arrived at the hospital with the day's mail.

The answer was sometimes surprising. Strangers sent money. Paper cranes. A soft blanket. Star Wars stickers. A drawing of a

TARDIS from *Doctor Who*. A four-page play written in Spanish. A book of poems by E. E. Cummings.

A friend from the live-action role-playing community sewed Sasha a skirt and matching vest.

The East Bay Heritage Quilters sent a vibrant purple quilt.

People from the conlang community sent letters in their invented languages using beautiful calligraphy.

People from Canada sent things with maple leaves on them.

High school Gay-Straight Alliances from all over the country sent cards decorated with rainbows.

The missives piled up – handmade cards, shop-bought cards, folded sheets of notebook paper, emails. They came from Colombia, Germany, France, Australia. *Get well*, they said. *Stay strong. Be proud. You are beautiful the way you are.*

Sasha couldn't concentrate on any of it for long, but they liked knowing that so many people cared. Cards from Sasha's friends stayed in the hospital room. So did the bouquet of silk flowers. Everything else, Debbie and Karl took home.

Over the next few weeks, Debbie would periodically type Sasha's name into Google to see how the story was being covered around the world. Once, the search led her to a neo-Nazi site.

'They were having a really hard time,' she said. 'An African American? *Oh, evil!* But then it's this trans kid wearing a skirt. What?'

'They couldn't figure out who to root against,' Karl explained. He grinned. 'It was a really hard time for the neo-Nazi community.'

Nobody who knew him could believe it. Richard was a goofball, sure, but hateful? It just didn't make sense.

'It blew me back,' Carlitta Collins, the school security officer, said. 'It blew my weave back to the fat part.'

Word was that Richard had set the skirt alight at the urging of another kid. Got played. Fell for the okie-doke. 'I just couldn't understand why he would make such a childish mistake,' Collins said. 'But then I thought about it. Like, "Oh, he's sixteen."'

But that wasn't how the rest of the school saw it. Richard had only been there for two months, and he didn't know too many people. For most students, all that mattered was that O High was in the news again, and not for any of the good things that happened there. It was like nobody ever paid attention until somebody screwed up.

'He was black and he did that. Most of us that go here are black. We're expected to do something wrong,' explains Emarieay, who played on the football and baseball teams. 'People act like, if you go to O High, that's the baddest school in Oakland. Since that happened, people just thought that all of us are basically the same.' It was important to say no. To say, that's not us. 'What our student allegedly did to Sasha is hideous and is not representative of the values we know to be true of the Oakland High community,' principal Matin Abdel-Qawi said in a letter he read over the school loudspeaker. 'We are all capable of doing what is right even and especially when it seems impossible. We all have a responsibility to stop acts of violence … The student body at Oakland High is extremely diverse. Our families come from all over the world. Wouldn't it be amazing if we led by example and showed Oakland what it means to respect and appreciate each other's differences?'

A movement sprouted on campus: No H8. Students and staff painted banners that said SASHA WE STAND WITH YOU. A student-led fundraiser collected more than $800 for Sasha's medical bills. Students folded a long chain of paper cranes and sent it to Sasha. In December, O High's Wildcats basketball team played its first home game wearing blue jerseys with Sasha's name on the back and the words *No H8* on the front. The gymnasium was festooned with handmade posters in the blue and white Wildcat colours that said NOT IN OUR SCHOOL and STAND UP TO HATE.

A number of the boys on the basketball team knew Richard, and they had come to practice after his arrest talking about what happened. Richard wasn't a bad kid, they said, just a follower. It seemed wrong that he might be locked up for life. But then one of the players pointed out that they should be thinking about the victim too. What happened to Sasha was horrible. 'That shouldn't happen to *anybody*,' he said. 'What if that had happened to somebody in *your* family?' That was when the team decided to order jerseys that stood up for Sasha.

'We're against hate and bullying,' basketball coach Orlando Watkins said when the team gathered in the locker room before the game, wearing their *No H8* jerseys. 'This is a big game for us today, not just because we need the victory, but it represents something bigger than just basketball. So let's go out there today, let's play hard, let's stay focused, and let's take care of business.' The team listened somberly, then gathered in a circle.

'No hate on me! No hate on three!' team captain Keith called. 'One, two, three ...'

'No hate!'

Kaprice found it hard to go to school. In her time in the Oakland schools she'd seen plenty of kids drop out or get kicked out, get shot, or get pregnant. But Richard was supposed to be different.

'I can't even hardly express the feelings I have, because I knew where he was trying to go,' she says. 'I knew he would be the one graduating from here.'

The NO H8 banners were everywhere, but no one was talking about Richard. Abdel-Qawi, the school principal, had concluded the letter he read over the loudspeaker by reminding students to 'show our student, currently in custody, compassion and tolerance.' But Richard's friends felt that this last bit had been plastered over by the reams of NO H8 posters. One by one, they showed up in Kaprice's office to complain.

'They said it was a hate crime, but he had family that wasn't straight,' Richard's friend Lidell said. 'We were with "No H8" but in Richard's case it wasn't hate. What he did was wrong, as like a joke, playful. It was like a funny little prank-joke turns to something that ends your whole life.'

To Lidell, it just seemed like the outside world didn't grasp how easy it was for kids who grew up in poor neighbourhoods to take that wrong turn.

'People have different habitats,' he explained. 'Some people have it better than others. They grew up in good neighbourhoods. Their family has jobs. They have good income. They don't understand. Their life is so good, they think *everybody's* life is good. They don't understand the struggles people go through. I don't know where you grew up at, if it's like a low-income area, where there's a lot of violence and crime. But if you grew up in a low-income area and all you see is crime and drugs? If you have family that does crime? You see it. It has an impact on you. If you're around it a lot, it's hard to do good.'

'It just hurt,' Cherie said. 'Somebody you are that close to? And it becomes, like, all viral?' She shook her head. 'People would say all type of stuff. Like he was just intentionally trying to burn him. Like, "Oh yeah, he gay, he hecka gay, let's burn him." I'm not saying what he did was right, I'm just saying at the end of the day, he was sixteen. You're all just trying to put an opinion on something that you don't know. Y'all don't know.'

THE CIRCLE

Each day that the No H8 organising at Oakland High School went on, Richard's friends grew increasingly upset. Finally, Kaprice went to Principal Abdel-Qawi to ask if she could hold a restorative justice circle so that Richard's friends could share their feelings. She invited Amy Wilder, an Oakland High School resource specialist who was the faculty adviser for the school's Gay-Straight Alliance. Wilder, who majored in gender studies in college, had been working with students to show support for Sasha.

About a dozen students gathered in a circle in an empty classroom a few days later. Most of them didn't really know each other – Richard was the one thing they had in common. The facilitator passed around a green racing car that served as a 'talking piece.' When the racing car reached you, it was your turn to speak. Otherwise, you listened.

The first few times the racing car went around the circle the questions were playful. *If you were a superhero, what would your superpower be?* Questions that let them get to know one another a bit. Then they talked about Richard. How silly he was, and how kind, and how he'd had a friend and a family member who were gay. One of them passed around a photo of Richard on a mobile phone.

When the phone reached Wilder, she gave a start of recognition. It was Richard's eyes she remembered. His hazel eyes.

Earlier in the year, a parent had come in to meet with her and had brought along a younger sibling. The kid was wild, out of control. No way were they going to be able to have a conversation with this kid bouncing off the walls. But then Richard had come out of Kaprice's office. He went over to the kid and somehow calmed him down, got him focused so the meeting could take place.

Now, as she stared at Richard's picture, Wilder's eyes filled with tears. 'Because he was so sweet,' she explained. 'And he's such a young person facing such serious consequences.'

'When she shared that, it was huge,' Kaprice said afterwards. 'It was incredible. We could hardly take it.'

All they had wanted was someone else to understand.

SKINNED

Five days after the second surgery, Sasha returned to the operating theatre, where Dr Grossman's team used a tool called a Dermatome to harvest three-inch-wide strips of skin from Sasha's back. After removing each strip, Dr Grossman passed it through a meshing device that perforated it with tiny holes so that it could be stretched to cover a larger area. Then he placed it over Sasha's wounds and stapled it into place. Peel, mesh, place, staple. Peel, mesh, place, staple. When it was over, the burn sites were covered with new skin. But Sasha's back was raw, exposed. The pain was intense – more intense than the burns had been. It was as if they had been skinned alive.

GOD IS GOOD

The Ladies seemed to materialise out of nowhere. There were three of them at the third court hearing on 26 November, older white women who dressed as chastely as nuns, in polo necks and blazers and sensible shoes. They came, they said, because they were concerned about Richard.

'Not that it's not a horrible crime,' one explained, 'but it's also a crime to try a child as an adult.'

Inside the courtroom, defendants appeared in a small box to the left of the judge. It was possible to see them only if you sat on the far right side of the gallery and pressed your cheek against the wall. By the third hearing, the reporters had figured this out and they all squished into the same column of seats, leaning into one another to get a glimpse of Richard's face.

Jasmine wore glossy pink lipstick, black leggings and a T-shirt that said *Los Angeles*. Her face was bright, eager, confident. She knew it would all turn out OK.

'God is good,' she repeated to herself in the lift. 'God is good. God is so good.'

'You look nice,' her cousin Regis said as the family gathered in the hallway, waiting for Du Bois to be done talking to reporters. 'I like your hair.' His own hair was gorgeous – streaked red and gold, with hair extensions he'd made himself. He was dressed stylishly in a gold jacket, tight jeans, a scarf and lace-up boots. They were an attractive trio, he and Jasmine and Jasmine's sister Juliette. As they waited for Richard's lawyer to give them an update, they talked about what they were cooking for Thanksgiving, just two days away. Macaroni and cheese. Yams. That spinach dip they loved.

Conversation turned to a case that was in the news – Donald Williams Jr, an African American in his first year at San Jose State University, had been relentlessly bullied by the white students he lived with in a four-bedroom dormitory suite. The white kids, also in their first year, had insisted on calling Williams 'three-fifths,' a reference to the clause in the original US Constitution that counted slaves as three-fifths of a person when determining population for representation in Congress. They clamped a bike lock around his neck and claimed to have lost the key. They wrote *Nigger* on a whiteboard and draped a Confederate flag over a cardboard cutout of Elvis Presley in the suite's living room. They locked him in his room. And they claimed it was all just a series of good-natured pranks.

In the end, three eighteen-year-old white students were expelled for what they did to Williams, and a seventeen-year-old was suspended. The three who were expelled were also charged in criminal court. The charge: misdemeanour battery with a hate-crime enhancement, which carried a maximum penalty of a year and a half in county jail. A jury eventually convicted all three of battery but acquitted one of the students of the hate-crime charge and deadlocked on the others.

'Girl, they got *misdemeanours*,' Regis said. 'Nobody got charged with any felonies. Three white boys on one black boy.'

Sasha was released from hospital the next day, twenty-three days after the fire. Reporters lined the street in front of Sasha's house, pushing up against the front door. News helicopters circled.

Sasha gave an interview to the local news, wearing a skirt over bandaged legs. 'I was really excited that an agender person was in the news,' they said later. 'But I wasn't that excited about the circumstances, obviously. Those were my feelings: This is really great – but does it have to be me?'

Sasha also suspected that not everyone understood what the story was all about. 'I got the idea that it wasn't really about me being agender,' they said. 'A lot of the news coverage was, "A boy was wearing a skirt." Rather than, "An agender person was wearing a skirt." And that kind of bugged me, that I was being misrepresented in that way.'

Sasha returned to school in December, on the Monday after
the Thanksgiving break. They were eager to be back after the long
boring days in hospital and they dressed a little smarter than
usual – matching the flat cap and skirt with a vest, bow tie and
crisp white shirt. The press was there, of course – craning to get a
view of Sasha, like paparazzi angling for a shot of the royal family.

Sasha's friends made a point of not making a big deal about
Sasha's return, and they asked their classmates to do the same.
They knew Sasha hated being the centre of attention, so after
greeting them with hugs they tried to be chill. As chill as you can
be with a line of news trucks idling in front of your school, antennae
stabbing the sky.

'There were so many cameras at the school and they were like,
"Are you Sasha's friend, can we talk to you?"' Teah remembered.

'And that was a little weird because I didn't know how to approach my friendship with Sasha. I don't think Sasha wanted to be around their friends with their friends thinking, "I'm talking to a famous person," or "I'm talking to somebody that something horrible happened to." They just wanted things to be normal. It really distanced me from the friendship, which is a shame.'

After school, Sasha went to Ballroom Dance Club. Teah was crazy about ballroom dancing, so she had started the club and Sasha, Nemo and Michael had joined. Sasha and Nemo were useful additions, because they could dance either the male or the female part, depending on what was needed. That first day back, Sasha waltzed with Michael as their partner. Michael noticed that his friend was quieter than they'd been before. A little more inward. But overall Sasha seemed OK.

WORST DAYS EVER

There were a lot more of them now. Worst Days. Worst Nights. The days their legs itched from the graft, from their leg hairs getting caught in the bandages, a prickly irritation that never stopped. The days their legs ached. When everything that used to be normal was suddenly difficult: showering (seated now, using a handheld shower), getting dressed (both legs had to be wrapped in three layers of bandages), going to school (they were so tired, just so very tired). The nights after getting home from the hospital when they felt like they had to pee all the time, but couldn't, a side effect of having had a urinary catheter in for all those weeks in the hospital. The nights when sleep felt like a distant cousin they'd met long ago but didn't know well enough to talk to. The nights they took medication for the pain and it made them hyper instead of sleepy.

They tried not to think about the fire or the person who set it, but sometimes it was hard not to wonder why, not to just feel incredulous that this was the situation – one minute you're on your way home from school and then it's an ambulance and a hospital and surgery and pain and painkillers and bandages and seated showers. It was just like, *How is this a thing that happens?*

REUNION

Dan Gale sat in a wicker chair in Sasha's living room beside his cousin Russell, taking deep, nervous breaths and exhaling through his teeth. It was a Saturday in early December and Dan had been invited to join Sasha's family for brunch. Russell came along for support.

The past few weeks had been a whirlwind for Dan. A month ago he'd been an ordinary guy, a construction worker who did some extra work on the side at a friend's T-shirt shop. Then he'd taken the bus home from work one day and helped save the life of a teenager whose skirt was on fire. Suddenly he was a hero, a Good Samaritan. He'd been honored at City Hall, featured on the news. Police chief Sean Whent had said that Dan's actions on the bus had proved that despite Oakland's reputation for crime, 'there are good people all over the city.' Even his own family looked at him with a newfound respect.

Now Dan was about to see Sasha for the first time since that day on the bus. But it was taking Sasha a while to come out of their bedroom.

'They have to put these stockings on over the scars,' Debbie explained. 'There are a few spots that still have to be bandaged, but they're healing really well.'

'That's great,' Dan said, his expression grave. He was in his early fifties and had basset-hound brown eyes, a thick salt-and-pepper moustache and a deep, gravelly voice. He crossed and uncrossed his legs, resting one of his white tennis shoes on his knee. Beside him, Russell, who owned the construction company where Dan worked, blinked sleepily, a three-day beard peppering his cheeks. The two of them surveyed the living room, which was cozy and cluttered, its surfaces covered with houseplants, magazines, dried flowers and framed photographs, its shelves overflowing with hardback books and board games, its limited floor space crammed with musical instruments (a piano, two guitars, a bongo drum). A paper banner inscribed with get-well messages wrapped nearly all the way around the room, a souvenir from the march along the 57 bus route the previous month.

At last Sasha came in, wearing a gray hoodie and a black skirt, legs swaddled in white bandages.

Dan sucked in a breath.

'Oh, wow,' he whispered. He stood and enveloped Sasha in a hug. 'How you doing, man?'

'I'm doing good.' Sasha blinked a few times, grinning shyly.

'You look great.'

'Yeah. I'm not feeling too bad.'

'That's great. Don't change who you are, dude, don't change.' Dan shook his head. 'This is weird. Awkward.' His eyes brimmed with tears. 'I'm sorry, dude. I'm really sorry,' he croaked, voice breaking.

'Thanks for all you did,' Karl said, coming into the room behind Sasha.

'Man, I'm sorry I couldn't've done more.' Dan turned to Sasha. 'It was hard to get to you.'

'You did all you could,' Sasha said. 'You did the best—'

But Dan had already moved on to the future. He wanted to accompany Sasha on their return to the bus. 'I want to be there,' he insisted. 'I mean, you're my friend now. Forever. Because of you, because of this whole situation, I feel real better about myself. I have a better relationship with my daughters and stuff. I'm *sorry* for what happened to you. But man, I benefited big-time out of it.' He laughed and, to his evident relief, everyone joined in.

The conversation moved in fits and spurts – lapsing into awkward pauses and then reigniting again. Sasha told Dan about using the fire to full advantage. '"I can't do the dishes, my legs got injured." "I can't help with dinner, my legs!" "I can't do my homework – legs!"'

Dan talked about how he'd seen Sasha on the bus for years, always with a book in hand. 'The kid's smarter than everybody on the bus combined,' he announced. Then he turned back to Sasha. 'That's because of your parents, you know. Remember this: all your life you're going to want your parents off your back. Then you realise when you get older, they're the only ones that *had* your back.'

'*You* had my back,' Sasha said.

Dan shut his eyes for a moment.

'You know, I turned around and I saw the fire,' he said. 'And my first reaction was, "Oh, I can do this. I got this."'

Twenty years earlier, he explained, he'd been with a friend who was driving a car at a demolition derby. The friend had been working on the car when he mistook a container of petrol for a container of water and tried to use it to douse a spark. When Dan saw his friend go up in flames, he tackled him and put him out. Who'd ever imagine it was a skill he'd need to use a second time?

Over breakfast – a tofu scramble for Sasha, eggs and pastries for everyone else – the conversation turned to the kid who'd set Sasha on fire. Debbie and Karl had told reporters that they wanted to see Richard tried as a juvenile, not as an adult.

'I think you guys are a lot more lenient about what you want to see than I would be,' Dan said.

'Mostly, it's just – we don't know,' Karl explained. They didn't want to be the ones to decide what should happen to Richard. They didn't feel like they had enough information. 'I'll leave it to other people to figure out.'

Dan turned to Sasha. 'How do *you* feel on that? I mean, this kid *hurt* you.'

Sasha considered this. 'I know he hurt me. He did something that's really dangerous and stupid. But then again, he's a sixteen-year-old kid and sixteen-year-old kids are kind of dumb. It's really hard to know what I want for him.'

PART 4

JUSTICE

BINARY

There are two kinds of people in the world.

Male and Female.

Gay and Straight.

Black and White.

Normal and Weird.

Cis and Trans.

There are two kinds of people in the world.

Saints and Sinners.

Victims and Villains.

Cruel and Kind.

Guilty and Innocent.

There are two kinds of people in the world.

Just two.

Just two.

Only two.

Jasmine had her eyes fixed on Richard as he was escorted into the courtroom. He was dressed in Juvenile Hall's gray sweatshirt and khaki trousers, his hair cropped close. When his eyes landed on her face, she made the shape of a heart with her fingers and held it to her chest.

He grinned, then he pulled his expression into a neutral mask. If he smiled, people might think he didn't have compassion for Sasha. They might say he was smirking.

It was mid-January. Richard had been at Juvenile Hall for over two months. So far, not much had happened on his case. But today, a judge would hear a petition Du Bois had filed asking the judge to send Richard's case back to juvenile court.

Proposition 21, the law allowing prosecutors to file charges against juveniles in adult court, had been upheld by the California Supreme Court way back in 2002. But three subsequent United States Supreme Court decisions had put strict limits on the sentences that juveniles can receive, eliminating death sentences and many sentences of life without the possibility of parole, sometimes called LWOP. In each case, the high court had cited the Eighth Amendment to the US Constitution, which bans 'cruel and unusual' punishment.

Richard hadn't killed anybody, so he wasn't facing the death penalty or life without the possibility of parole. If he received a life sentence, he'd be eligible to go before the parole board in seven years. But Du Bois argued that the Supreme Court decisions about the death penalty and LWOP indicated 'evolving standards of decency' that made it increasingly unacceptable to impose harsh sentences on young offenders.

'Proposition 21 enabled the DA – a criminal prosecutor by trade – to unilaterally decide at the outset of any proceedings that the 16-year-old Defendant was *irredeemably* a depraved "criminal" offender who should be *permanently* deprived of the rehabilitative and parental reunification objectives and treatment originally provided to all … juvenile offenders,' he wrote.

None of this made much of an impression on Judge Richard Couzens. He pointed out that Richard hadn't yet been tried, which made it too early to weigh in on the constitutionality of any sentence he might receive. And, he added, 'This conduct is very egregious and I don't think anybody would argue that if it were committed by an adult that the punishment would be cruel and unusual.'

The petition was denied.

In the hall outside the courtroom, Jasmine wept in her sister Juliette's arms. She took the lift down to the lobby with her eyes fastened on the floor.

'He's my baby,' she said softly. 'All I can do is stand by him.'

The staff at Juvenile Hall remembered Richard from his previous stay there when he was fourteen, before he was sent to the group home. He'd been a pain in the ass then – the kind of kid who kept asking for things, and if he didn't get what he wanted, he'd ask someone else. He took up a lot of time, but they'd liked him anyway.

'He was never a bad kid,' one staffer explained. 'He's just a needy kid.'

He seemed different now. The goofy, antic quality was gone. These days, Richard was serious. Withdrawn. The boys who knew him before said he'd gotten boring. He didn't care about getting laughs.

There were just ninety or a hundred kids in all of Juvenile Hall, most of them boys, even though the facility had been built for three hundred and sixty. Now, with juvenile incarceration rates sinking, only half of the twelve thirty-bed units were open, and each of those was only half full.

Richard knew the Juvenile Hall routine already. Before you leave your room in the morning, fold up your pajamas and blankets and leave them in a neat pile on the bed, what they called 'open-air style.' Step outside, put your shoes on, and then stand in front of your cell with your hands clasped behind your back to await instructions. Breakfast is in the common area, at one of the round tables with checked patterns in the centre. School is a few yards away, in two classrooms next to the common area.

Those classrooms were the most colourful part of the unit, the walls covered with posters, word lists, number lines – a visual vacation from the drab sameness of the rest of the unit. Richard found it was easier to concentrate there than it had been at school, even with the chaos of the living unit occasionally erupting outside the classroom door. He steadily moved through his coursework, earning decent grades for the first time in his high school career.

On Sundays he went to services, which were held inside one of the classrooms. He liked studying the Bible, particularly the story of Job. In the story, God tests Job's faith by killing his wife and his children and his servants, destroying his house, his animals and all his possessions. He makes Job's skin erupt in boils. Eventually Job is reduced to nothing but raw suffering. 'How is this fair?' Job asks. 'What kind of God does this to people?'

At the end of the story, God comes to Job in a whirlwind to answer his questions with questions of his own. 'Would you discredit my justice? Would you condemn *me* to justify *yourself*?'

he asks. He asks Job if he was there when the earth was made, if he knows where light and darkness dwell, if he can bind a unicorn and make him plow the field. 'Do you have an arm like God's, and can your voice thunder like his?'

'Okay,' Job says. 'I see your point. God's knowledge and power are so vast, there's no point in questioning his choices.' For Richard, the story was a comfort.

Early on in his stay, Richard found himself sharing a fifteen-person living unit with the kid who had robbed him at gunpoint, the one he had thought of as a friend. The boy apologised for robbing him. Richard told Jasmine that he'd accepted the apology because he knew what it was like to have wronged somebody. He, too, hoped to be forgiven.

'Forgive, but don't forget,' Jasmine liked to say. But now Richard told her to stop saying that.

'To forgive, you *have* to forget,' he counselled. 'Because otherwise you haven't truly forgiven.'

Jasmine tried to stay focused on the positive. Richard was going to learn from this experience, she was sure. 'We're *all* going to learn something from this,' she said frequently. But once, after saying it, she shook her head.

'I wish it hadn't gone this far and he could have learned a different way,' she said. 'I wish that the courts would give him a suitable punishment so that he can learn from this instead of just being institutionalised.'

Sometimes, her mind couldn't help flicking through an ever-changing list of what-ifs. What if she'd been able to afford to pay a lawyer to defend Richard when he was fourteen instead of letting him be represented by the public defender? What if she had had him tested for ADHD when he was in his first year of high school, like she'd thought about doing? What if she'd been able to find a place to live outside of Oakland, where there weren't so many bad influences? What if he'd had more activities in his life, more things to keep him out of trouble? What if she'd taken him to sign up for an after-school jobs programme like he'd been asking? What if Richard had called her when he was first arrested instead of talking to the police? What if she'd gone down to the police station when she first saw him on the news? She should have gone down there instead of calling. She shouldn't have just taken their word for it when they told her they didn't know anything. She should have—

But then she'd stop herself. There had to be a reason why all of this was turning out the way it had.

'God works in mysterious ways,' she said. 'He don't do anything on accident. Everything he do, he know exactly what he's doing.'

NOT READY

Christmas came and went. School started again. Sasha was accepted into the Massachusetts Institute of Technology. By February life had slipped back toward normality – a new normal, in which Sasha's legs were bound in white compression stockings twenty-three hours a day to prevent the development of thick scars at the site of the skin grafts. The compression stockings were more comfortable than the bandages had been, and Sasha's atrophied leg muscles had regained their strength.

Jasmine wanted to meet with Sasha's family. She'd been thinking about it since Richard was first arrested. She wanted to tell them how sorry she was, mother to mother, parent to parent.

'I can imagine if it was my baby,' she said. 'He didn't do anything for that to be done to him.'

But when Debbie heard the idea, she flinched. She thought about Jasmine often, she said, and she believed in forgiveness. But it was just too soon. She needed more time.

Richard's first evidentiary hearing was in March. Sasha took the day off from school and came to court with Karl and Debbie, dressed in a navy blue skirt, a gray vest, a brown striped bow tie, a gray flat cap, a trench coat, purple leggings and purple high-tops. They carried a book about the history of American socialism.

Jasmine stared at Sasha, whom she was seeing in person for the first time. Emotions swirled inside her. Sorrow and compassion. Confusion and shame. Emptiness.

The hearing was over in minutes. Richard was 'held to answer,' which meant that there was enough evidence against him for a judge to set a date for trial. As Sasha's family filed out of the courtroom, Jasmine dashed over to speak to them.

'My son's not like that,' she said, the words tumbling out of her mouth in a rush. 'I don't know what made him do that, and I'm sorry. We're not hateful people.'

Then she hugged each member of the family: Debbie, Karl, Sasha.

One by one, each of Richard's relatives came forward to do the same.

When it was over, both mothers were crying. Jasmine kept talking about Sasha. 'He just looked so innocent,' she said. 'He's just so cute. He has such a nice family. It's just not something I can get used to.'

There was so much more she had wanted to say, but she couldn't find the words. 'I don't know what to say but sorry.'

In the lift, Debbie wiped away tears. 'I felt like it was genuine on their part,' she said. 'It was good. I'm really glad. It was worth coming here today just for that.'

When asked how it had felt to be hugged by the family of the person who had set them on fire, Sasha just smiled.

'I'm always okay with hugs,' they said.

Afterwards, Karl, Debbie and Sasha took the courthouse lift to the ninth floor to meet with Armando Pastran, the deputy district attorney who was prosecuting the case.

Pastran had seen the two families embrace, but he seemed unmoved.

'I'm glad that *they* showed some remorse,' he said of Richard's family. 'I'd like to see some from the person who did it.'

Pastran had never spoken to Richard, of course. That's not how the system works. And Richard's letters were still tucked away in his lawyer's briefcase.

A year after Sasha first posted their nonbinary gender petition, another petition went up on the We the People website. The wording was pretty much identical to the one Sasha had written.

This time, the petition went viral, attracting attention from Reddit, *Bustle*, the *Advocate* and *Huffington Post*. It earned 103,202 signatures and an official White House response, which said, in part, 'We know how important this issue is, and we understand the profound impact, both symbolic and otherwise, of having official documents that accurately reflect an individual's identity ... We cannot overstate the care and seriousness that should be brought to bear on the issue.'

That didn't mean the White House was planning to change federal policy. The official statement said that proposals to change the way gender is listed on government documents 'should be considered on a case-by-case basis by the affected federal and state agencies.' Still, Sasha felt proud. The government had acknowledged the existence of nonbinary gender. Who would have thought it possible?

PRETTY

Michael's girlfriend, Teah, stood behind Sasha, yanking at the laces of a scarlet corset.

'I wonder, if I keep pulling, if Sasha will just disappear into negative space,' she mused.

It was April. She and Michael and Sasha and Nemo were getting ready for the Gaskell Ball, a Victorian gathering held in downtown Oakland at the Scottish Rite Center, an ornate 1920s-era building on the shores of Lake Merritt. Teah's mother, Alisa Foster, is a costume designer. She had made Sasha a ball gown as a gift, using fabric donated by the Sisters of Perpetual Indulgence, a San Francisco charity and street performance group that calls itself 'a leading-edge Order of queer nuns.' The dress had a twenty-three-inch waist. Teah, whose own gown was olive green and trimmed with gold ruffles, measured Sasha's waist. Just under twenty-five inches. She yanked harder at the corset strings.

'Sasha, how are you even alive currently?' Michael asked. He was wearing a gray vest and trousers and a burgundy bow tie.

'Magic.' Sasha grinned. They tapped their own collarbones. 'My lungs are up here. The human body is a wondrous thing.'

'I feel a little bit guilty – I'm suffocating you,' Teah said, pulling the corset tighter.

'It's consensual,' Sasha said. 'Anyway, I don't think that's suffocation. Suffocation is when you put a pillow over someone's mouth and nose.'

Just then, Nemo walked in, wearing an Edwardian waistcoat, pleated black trousers, a starched white shirt and a cravat patterned in blue and gray. They had pulled their straight brown hair into a ponytail at the nape of their neck.

'The curves are a good look for you,' Nemo deadpanned, taking in Sasha's hourglass shape.

Nemo sat down on the couch beside Teah and Michael and watched as Teah's mother helped Sasha into a royal-blue ball gown with a scooped neck and leg-of-mutton sleeves. A matching blue headpiece rested in Sasha's hair, a silk rosette over each ear.

'I feel pretty!' Sasha announced, twirling in front of the mirror.

'You're so beautiful!' Nemo said, conducting Sasha in a brief waltz around the room. 'Oh my God!'

Sasha was too tightly bound by the corset to put on shoes, so Nemo sat on the floor to do it for them.

Mitzi, Teah's small black dog, sniffed at the hem of Sasha's dress.

'Dog,' Sasha said irritably. 'I'm dry-clean only.'

'*You're* dry-clean only?' Nemo inquired. 'Or your dress?'

'Well, I effectively *am* my dress,' Sasha observed. 'On the outside.'

'Are you?' Nemo asked, interested by the statement. 'But you're also your skin and your necklace.'

Sasha shrugged. 'The parts of me that are accessible to the dog are dry-clean only.'

They entered together, hand in hand, forearm to forearm. The ballroom's wooden floor gleamed under their feet. The revellers promenaded in pairs, women in bustled ball gowns in bright candy colours, men in frock coats with waxed moustaches. The outfits were a mash-up of eras and styles – long gloves and short ones, feathers and jewels, flapper dresses, miniskirts, suits, jeans and at least one man in a kilt with a raccoon-pelt pouch at his waist.

This is it, Sasha thought. I'm here in my ball gown, with my partner, and it's wonderful.

It was wonderful because the dress was pretty and Sasha was pretty and the room was pretty and Nemo was pretty. It was wonderful because Sasha loved ballroom dancing. And it was wonderful because for that night at least, nobody was going to mistake Sasha for a boy. All evening, men asked Sasha to dance.

'What I want is for people to be confused about what gender I am,' Sasha explained later. That didn't happen too often – people tended to see Sasha as male. So it was a nice change to be seen as female.

On the stage, a brass band struck up an oompah-pah waltz. Sasha and Nemo danced.

Darris Young worked as an organiser for an Oakland social justice advocacy group called the Ella Baker Center for Human Rights. He had been hired while still on probation after doing time, and he was passionate about keeping young people out of prison.

'I did seventeen years, two days, four hours and twenty minutes on a twenty-year sentence as a third striker,' he explained in an interview posted on the Ella Baker Center's website. 'I saw a lot of things that were wrong with the system. Especially, as I started to see the years go by, the people that were coming in were getting younger and younger, and I was like: there's something wrong with this. Why are we sending kids to prison for things that maybe they should have gotten corrected in their lives? And then I saw a pattern that most of them had started out in the juvenile justice system, which let me know that somewhere down the line, it was failing.'

Darris had followed Richard's case in the news. When he saw Sasha's family on TV saying that they wanted Richard to be charged as a juvenile, he felt there was a chance that maybe a different kind of solution could be reached, one that didn't involve sending Richard to prison.

'Here was a case where so many people thought, OK, yeah, it's a horrific thing that happened, but yet here's a young man that seemed to be salvageable – he didn't have a long criminal record or anything like that,' he said. 'Especially because the victim's family, they were so forgiving. It seemed like they just wanted to put this behind them without causing any more harm to the community at large, because, you know, whenever anyone goes to prison it harms the whole community, it has ripple effects up and down.'

Darris and another organiser, Maria Dominguez, contacted Jasmine to see if she might be interested in something called restorative justice. Jasmine wasn't interested at first – she'd never heard of restorative justice, and she was already feeling overwhelmed. But eventually she agreed to meet with them to learn more. They couldn't promise anything – all the parties would have to agree, including Sasha's family, the district attorney, and Richard's defense lawyer, Bill Du Bois. But they knew that a restorative justice advocate named Anna Blackshaw had been in touch with Sasha's family, and so they thought it might be possible to bring the two sides together to keep Richard out of prison.

'Once you send an eighteen-year-old to state prison, there are older individuals there and they are very influential,' Darris explained. 'Most of the time, individuals don't come out of prison better.'

One day in the autumn of 2015, two 14-year-old students sat in Biology class at Oakland High School watching a substitute teacher try in vain to control the classroom. The two could not have been more different. TC was soft-spoken, slight and of Vietnamese descent. She dressed like most Oakland High students, in a hoodie and sweats, but she wore her long black hair in two girlish braids. Jeff was a rambunctious African American boy with a blonde streak in his close-cropped hair. The kind of kid who talks nonstop, unleashing a stream of comic commentary that's half hilarious, half annoying. The kind of kid who, when the girl at the desk next to him doesn't want to show him her folder, slaps her hard on the behind.

The smack caught TC entirely by surprise. It hurt and it was humiliating. Nobody had ever touched her butt before. Furious, she picked up a chair, ready to hurl it at Jeff.

The classroom erupted into commentary and instructions. 'Put it down!' a classmate urged.

'If you don't know anything about it, you need to shut the fuck up!'

TC shouted, her eyes filling with tears. But she put the chair down.

The event stayed with her all day. That afternoon she told some of her friends what had happened and began to cry.

'You need to report him,' they urged. So she did.

When Oakland High School administration began to investigate, they found that in the preceding couple of days, Jeff had slapped or grabbed the butts of two other girls as well.

Sexual harassment is grounds for suspension or expulsion. But keeping students from going to school is usually counterproductive, and suspensions have been shown to disproportionately target African American males. For that reason, many Oakland schools have been exploring a different approach to school discipline: restorative justice.

Given a choice between traditional discipline – which would probably have meant Saturday school – and participating in a restorative justice circle with the three girls he'd touched, Jeff chose restorative justice. Still, he went into the process annoyed. He'd just been playing around. Why was everyone making such a big deal about it?

'It was like, I'm gonna go in there with a bunch of females and talk about something that's a week old?' Jeff said later.

Two of the girls, J. and Pancha, had similar feelings. They'd been mad at the time, but whatever. It was history now. 'I wasn't really traumatised about it,' Pancha said.

Schools are all about rules. There are rules against sexual harassment, and those rules spell out what kinds of conduct are prohibited and what the punishment should be. Restorative justice, on the other hand, is more interested in relationships. A crime,

RJ advocates say, is not an act against a rule, it's an act against a person. When you harm somebody, you owe it to them to make things right. By making things right, you begin to heal your relationship with the community.

'Our system is focused on blame and punishment and not on healing and learning,' says Lauren Abramson, who founded the Community Conferencing Center in Baltimore, Maryland, one of the oldest and most widely respected RJ programmes in the US. 'There's a different way to deliver justice that's been proven in many cases to be more socially effective and more cost-effective.'

The Oakland High circle started out silly. Nobody except TC and the two adult facilitators could stop joking around. But when the three girls started to talk about their feelings about being touched, things suddenly got serious. Nobody minded playing around, the girls said, but in this case Jeff had crossed the line. In the end, the four students made an agreement to ask permission before touching each other, even in play. And then the whole thing was done. Over.

More than over actually. Now the four were friends.

'We all bonded from this experience,' J. explained as the four of them shared a bag of cashews a few months later. 'It helped us get the feelings we had *out*. And we trust each other. It was a good way to get the event just out of our heads.'

And of course, asking for permission had become a running joke.

'Can I touch your nuts?' Pancha asked, helping herself to the bag of cashews. The others snorted.

Without the circle, they said, the whole thing would have blown over, but the residue would have remained.

'I think it would still have been kinda weird if we didn't do the restorative justice circle,' TC said. 'At least for me.'

'Yeah,' J. said, 'because whenever you'd see that person, it would just be like …'

'He's the one who smacked my ass!' Jeff finished. He and Pancha acted out running into each other at the supermarket sometime in the distant future.

'Hey, I'm Jeff, from high school.'

'You're the one who smacked my ass!'

'I'm the one who smacked your ass!'

They cracked up. Jeff stuffed a handful of nuts into his mouth.

'Would you *please* close your mouth when you eat?' Pancha said, making a face.

Jeff shook his head solemnly. 'We're going to need another restorative justice circle.'

Then he grinned. 'We ain't never used to talk like this,' he said. 'I feel like I can tell them more now. I can trust these three.'

That was the thing about restorative justice. It allowed you to hold two things in your head at the same time – that butt-slapping was funny, and also that it wasn't. That asking permission to touch somebody was funny, but that you really didn't want to be touched by somebody who didn't ask. That the girls wanted Jeff to dial back the ass-smacking thing, but that they still liked joking around with him. That the whole thing wasn't a big deal, and that it kind of was.

That was what community was. All those layers of understanding.

RESTORATIVE JUSTICE

Sujatha Baliga had been getting calls from community activists from the moment Richard was arrested. As one of the foremost experts on restorative justice in the US, she was the one people turned to in situations like this, situations where healing seemed possible. And so Sujatha had called a few people she knew in the Alameda County district attorney's office to say that she was available to facilitate if the families were interested in initiating a restorative justice process.

'I don't cold-call crime victims ever,' she says. 'I'm not here to peddle restorative justice.'

Restorative justice is sometimes used in Alameda County as an alternative to criminal court for juveniles accused of felonies, a process known as diversion because the accused is diverted away from criminal court. When that happens, a local not-for-profit organisation facilitates a process called family group conferencing that includes the offender, the offender's family, and other important adults like teachers or pastors, as well as the victim and the victim's supporters and advocates. The structure is similar to the one involving Jeff, TC, Pancha, and J. at Oakland High School – the members of the circle talk about what happened, and then make a plan for how the harm can be repaired. When it's a criminal case, the plan contains measurable benchmarks. If the kid completes the plan and meets the benchmarks, no criminal charges are ever filed.

A recent study of the Community Conferencing Center, one of the oldest restorative justice programmes in the US, in Baltimore, Maryland, found that those who took part in the process were 60 per cent less likely to reoffend than those who went through the traditional legal process.

'RJ isn't a guarantee of leniency,' Baliga cautioned. 'It's about dispensing with punitiveness for its own sake and trying to produce an outcome that will be more healing for everyone involved.'

Still, Baliga knew that there was little hope of diverting Richard from the criminal justice system entirely. 'Given the severity of the harm to Sasha, we didn't expect that the DA would allow the case to be diverted to restorative justice,' she said.

But if anyone seemed right for restorative justice, it was these two families, who had already expressed compassion for one another. 'They were perfect candidates for this dialogue,' she said. 'All of them were such gorgeously enlightened, beautiful people.'

Debbie and Karl didn't feel much need for restorative justice. The impromptu encounter with Jasmine had felt healing, but Debbie didn't have any desire for another meeting. 'I don't know what I would get out of meeting with Richard,' she said. 'I'm kind of not wanting to do that.'

She was wary, too, about making any recommendation about what should happen to him, other than that he should be treated as a juvenile.

'I've never felt like I have enough information to know how to judge or think about this kid,' she said. 'I don't want to be begging for lenience and then have him go out and hurt someone else. But I also don't want him sent to adult prison.'

Mostly she just wanted to see the case wrapped up before Sasha left for college. The one thing she didn't want was for Sasha to have to fly back from Massachusetts in the middle of the term to testify at a trial.

'I don't want to go to trial,' she said. 'I really don't.'

Richard's lawyer, Bill Du Bois, thought the whole restorative justice discussion was a distraction. There was no way, he said, that the district attorney's office would go for it. 'Restorative justice has never been a consideration in this case,' he said. 'I love their programme, but I've already broached the subject. It's the farthest thing. It's an absurd suggestion.'

For their part, the district attorney's office said they had no objection to the families going through the restorative justice process if they wanted, but it wouldn't affect the amount of time Richard served.

'This was not a case where he was not going to be incarcerated,' Alameda County DA Nancy O'Malley said. 'We could not ignore what he did.'

The truth was, the legal system had its own unassailable logic, a logic that couldn't be shifted.

Guilty vs. innocent.

Prosecutor vs. defense attorney.

Victim vs. offender.

TIRED

Spring stretched into summer.

One court appearance followed another. Each time Richard's case was called, all that happened was that the judge set another court date. Both sides were hoping for a plea bargain, but as time went on Jasmine's shining optimism faded. She came to the courthouse looking grim and sat in the hallway with Maria Dominguez and Darris Young from the Ella Baker Center, waiting for Richard's case to be called. They were the people she trusted to explain to her what was going on.

She was tired of talking about the case. Tired of thinking about it. 'I work twelve, sometimes fourteen hours a day and when I come home I just want to go to sleep,' she said. Hunched on a bench in the hallway, she looked like a guttering candle, its flame buffeted by the wind.

The press didn't come to court anymore. But the Ladies did. They never missed an appearance.

PLEASE TURN OFF CELL PHONES AND PAGERS BEFORE ENTERING COURTROOM.
NO FOOD, DRINKS, OR GUM CHEWING ALLOWED IN COURTROOM.
NO EATING OR TALKING OR READING WHILE COURT IS IN SESSION.
NO TALKING OR LOITERING IN THE VESTIBULE.
NO COMMUNICATION WITH INMATES.

Department 11 is a way station, a courtroom you pass through on your way to somewhere else. It's the court where cases are put on the calendar for their first hearings, where plea bargains are accepted and sentences passed down. No trials happen here. It's a clearinghouse – crowded in the morning, nearly empty by lunch. Here the in-custody defendants sit in the jury box waiting for their cases to be called. Their hands are cuffed and they wear colour-coded jailhouse jumpsuits: yellow for maximum security, blue for minimum and red for administrative segregation, which is the official term for solitary confinement.

The lawyers file in and out of the courtroom, sauntering past the gate that separates the gallery from the court, ducking back into chambers to chat with the judge, making small talk with the bailiff and one another. They lean down to confer with their clients, go on and off the record, consult their calendars.

In the gallery, friends and family members sit and watch, the bewildered audience to a play performed in an unknown dialect of acronyms, Latin and Old English.

Every once in a while the bailiff barks at someone in the seats who has been talking while court was in session. 'If I have to warn you again, you're out of here and you're not going to be allowed to come back.' Grown-ups flinch like misbehaving kids, guiltily lapsing into silence.

When you spend some time in the courthouse, you start to recognise the people who didn't heed that first warning. They're the ones outside in the hallway, slumped on a bench, faces streaked with impotent tears.

MAYBE

It was August. Sasha was getting ready to leave for college. They were excited and a little nervous. The nerves mostly had to do with leaving the Bay Area bubble. 'Here, finding a bunch of queer people to be my friends isn't very hard,' Sasha explained. 'Whereas, at MIT, I'm going to have to work a little harder to seek out my people.'

The fire was becoming a more distant memory, even though Sasha still wore compression stockings. 'Apart from some scars, I'm all healed, basically,' Sasha said. It was hard for people to believe it, but Sasha didn't feel traumatised by what had happened. When the physical pain faded, the emotional pain did as well.

'I don't really feel hated,' Sasha explained. 'Especially since after I was attacked, the whole world was supporting me. I felt like one person hates me – maybe.'

SUITCASE

Sasha packed for college. They brought all the usual things: bedsheets and shower shoes, clothes hangers, an alarm clock. They packed a ukelele, too, and a packet of subway maps.

For clothes, they took button-up shirts, T-shirts, leg warmers, and all the skirts they owned. Two pairs of Converse. One pair of ballet flats. And, of course, hats. Seven of them, including a knit cap, a flat cap, a Russian *ushanka* hat, and a Chairman Mao hat with a red star on the forehead.

A few key books came along as well: a vegan cookbook, the novel *Trains and Lovers* by Alexander McCall Smith, *The Left Hand of Darkness* by Ursula K. Le Guin, a book about anarchism called *Black Flame*, and the novel *Orlando* by Virginia Woolf, about a poet who changes genders from male to female.

Only two souvenirs from the fire travelled with Sasha to MIT.

One was the compression garments. The other was the string of paper cranes that had been made by the students at Oakland High School.

A PRAYER

As she got ready for her only child to leave home, Debbie thought about the psychologist who had first diagnosed Sasha with Asperger's syndrome. The psychologist said he'd seen many children with autism over the years, and none of them had ever married. He had advised Debbie and Karl to lower their expectations for the future. With a little luck and some hard work, he predicted, Sasha might be able to hold down a low-level job doing data processing.

At the time, Sasha was seven years old.

Debbie and Karl had chosen not to work with that particular psychologist. And now, more than a decade later, Debbie couldn't help gloating a little. *Take that, Mr Doom and Gloom therapist!*

she wrote on her blog in a pair of posts celebrating Sasha's high school graduation.

> Now Sasha is off to MIT—MIT!!! This dreamer, this creator of imaginary languages and a whole world in which to speak it. This sweet, funny, sometimes annoying, sometimes brilliant, naïve child of mine … This child who is now an adult and about to launch, like a rocket blazing in beauty through the night sky to worlds unknown. May the blaze and blast be glorious, and the universe welcoming. And may Sasha feel all of our love like a glowing halo around them.

Sasha left for college. It was now September 2014, nearly a year after the fire, and still the case wasn't settled. When Richard was brought into court, his eyes scanned the courtroom, taking everything in. Other inmates slumped listlessly, staring at the floor or the ceiling, but Richard always had the same quality of alertness. He noted who was there in the gallery – particularly the three older white ladies who always sat together. The bailiff had pointed them out to him, noting that they never missed an appearance. Who were they?

The district attorney's office had made an offer for a plea

bargain. They would drop the mayhem charge and the hate-crime enhancements if Richard agreed to accept a five-year sentence on the assault charge. With credit for time served and good behaviour, the deal would mean Richard, now seventeen, would be released just before his twenty-first birthday. That meant that even though he was being charged as an adult, he could still serve his time in juvenile facilities.

Du Bois thought Richard should take the plea. 'Not a single one of us like the deal,' he said. 'It's just the best choice among the available alternatives.'

But communication between Du Bois and Jasmine had almost completely broken down. She didn't know what to believe or who to trust. Even if he took the deal, what guarantee was there that Richard wouldn't be sent to adult prison when he turned eighteen? She sat in the hallway outside Department 11 with her head down, her whole body a fist.

'Are we going to resolve this today?' Judge Paul Delucchi asked wearily when Richard's case was called. 'I know we have allegedly been on the cusp of that for months.'

'We still are,' Du Bois said. The judge asked the parties to return to court in a couple of weeks. If they hadn't come to a plea agreement by then, the case would go to trial on 8 December.

'I'm a little frustrated,' Debbie fumed as the case dragged on. 'I just want it to be done with.'

THE DEAL

Richard sat in Judge Paul Delucchi's courtroom with his left leg shackled to a wooden chair. He wore a gray county-issue sweatshirt and khakis, and while he had lost the terrified look of his early court appearances, his eyes remained wary.

It was 16 October 2014, eleven months and twelve days since the fire on the bus. That morning Richard had decided to take the deal. He'd do the five years. Now he was just waiting to enter his plea.

As always, he scanned the courtroom, taking in his surroundings. Jasmine sat on the left, wearing new long hair extensions with a greenish tint. Debbie and Karl sat in the row in front of her. Some people from the restorative justice groups were scattered nearby, including Anna Blackshaw and Darris Young. The Ladies were in their usual spot, in a row near the back. A few members of the press sat near the front.

Everyone had come to see the case reach its resolution. But that morning, the district attorney's office had abruptly withdrawn the five-year offer. Now they had a new proposition: seven years in state prison.

Du Bois broke the news to Jasmine in the vestibule outside the courtroom. She erupted in fury and dismay.

'No! No! *No!*' she yelled. 'I've been nice! I've been polite!'

But there was nothing she could do. The district attorney's office held all the cards. Take it or go to trial, Du Bois said they'd told him.

Du Bois pulled up a chair beside Richard to explain what had happened. As the news registered, Richard's head sank to his chest.

Jasmine sat up straight in her seat, her eyes fixed intently on her son. Richard turned and met her eyes. They stared at each other for a long, heartbreaking moment. When Richard turned back to face Du Bois, he tucked his head into his shoulder like a bird wrapping itself in its own wing. Jasmine covered her mouth with one hand, her fingers curled into a fist.

The bailiff unlocked Richard's shackles and he stood, moving with a defeated, dreamlike languor. He looked back at his mother one more time, his eyes swimming, his face pale. Then he bent down and signed the plea.

THE FINE PRINT

Under the terms of the deal, Richard's sentence could still be reduced to five years – if he successfully jumped through a series of hoops. Three months after his sentencing, the judge would receive an evaluation of his conduct at the Division of Juvenile Justice, as California's juvenile facilities are called. If his conduct was good and he was participating in the educational and rehabilitation programmes offered there, he would return to court for a second evaluation in another three months, just before his eighteenth birthday. If this second evaluation was also positive, the judge would resentence him to five years in state prison instead of seven, which would mean he could stay in a juvenile facility for the whole time he was incarcerated. But if either evaluation had a black mark on it, the seven-year sentence would stand. If it did, Richard would be transferred to an adult prison when he turned eighteen.

Du Bois was visibly furious. 'He's now thrown to the wolves,' he said when the hearing was over. Any number of scenarios could lead to a bad discipline report, he pointed out. Richard could be attacked by another inmate, or harassed by a sadistic staff member. Weeks later, he was still fuming. 'He'll do five years in adult prison if he gets *one* bad progress report,' he said. 'It's punitive. And for what? Protecting the community by making this kid into a *real* gangster?'

A STRUCTURED ENVIRONMENT

District attorney Nancy O'Malley was never able to fully explain why the offer changed at the last minute. But it was pretty clear that her deputies had simply lost patience.

'It kept getting continued and continued and continued and the result was that he sat in our facility without having meaningful treatment,' she said.

There were more services available in the state's Division of Juvenile Justice facilities than in the county's Juvenile Hall, she argued, and the sooner Richard was sentenced, the sooner he could take advantage of them. 'We need this young man, when he comes out of incarceration, not to get on a bus and set another person on fire,' she said.

Of course, if Richard wasn't resentenced before he turned eighteen, he wouldn't be in a DJJ facility for long. He'd be sent to an adult prison, where the choice of programmes was meagre. But O'Malley was confident that Richard would be able to meet the benchmarks she'd set.

'By all accounts he appears to be someone who – unfortunately for him – does well in a structured environment,' she said. 'But he's not going to live in a structured environment forever.'

That was the story as she saw it: Richard did well when he was confined and poorly when he wasn't. Clearly, then, the solution was to keep confining him.

Some of Richard's friends had reached the same conclusion. Not because they wanted to protect the world from Richard, but because they wanted to protect Richard from the world. The world they knew had so many dead-end streets, so many dangerous corners, and no clearly marked way out.

Richard's cousin Gerald remembered how Richard had been the summer he first got back from Redding. Full of ambition and resolve. 'He was telling me when he first got out that he was doing good and he was going to work and stuff,' Gerald said. 'He started falling off when he started going with the wrong people.'

Gerald never said who those wrong people were, but in the year between Richard's arrest and his sentencing, two of his old friends were arrested for separate but equally serious crimes – carjackings and home invasion robberies. They were both sentenced to five years in adult prison.

'I'm not saying jail is for everybody, but it probably could save his life because look where his people went,' Cherie said. 'He's not going to do everything his friends are going to do, but he would've gotten wrapped up in some of it.'

That was the dilemma all of them faced in one form or another. If your friends were on a dangerous path, adults told you to cast them aside. But without your friends, who could you trust? Who could you count on to have your back?

Richard returned to court in November for sentencing. Debbie and Karl were there, as were Jasmine and her sister Juliette. Lloyd was there too. It was the first time he had come to one of Richard's court appearances. When Richard saw his family there, a smile flickered across his face and then disappeared, like a snail retreating into its shell.

Debbie had been asked to give a victim-impact statement. She was ushered past the wooden bar that separated the gallery from the court and given a glass of water to clear her throat. Then she stood in front of Richard and read aloud a letter, her voice quavering.

'You attacked our child as they slept on a bus,' she began. 'Maybe you thought it was weird that Sasha was wearing a skirt.'

Richard's gaze stayed on her face as she described Sasha's

ordeal – the charred skin, the painful skin grafts, the hours of daily bandaging. His eyes filled with tears.

'We do not understand your actions,' Debbie went on. 'But we also think that hatred only leads to more hatred and anger. We don't want you to come out of prison full of hate. Following the incident, communities near and far affirmed Sasha's – and everyone's – right to not be harassed or hurt or bullied for how they dress, or whether they are gay or trans or agender. We truly hope that you will gain some understanding and empathy in the years to come. Maybe sometime in the future *you* will be the one coming to the aid of someone being bullied.'

Afterwards, Debbie and Karl spent about half an hour answering questions from the media. Then they walked out of the courthouse in the November sunshine and stopped for coffee at a nearby café. They were exhausted from talking to reporters, unsure whether to be relieved or distraught.

'I felt like it was important that he hear it from us,' Debbie said of the letter she'd read. 'What that was like. I don't want people to think, Oh, it's not a big deal to us because we've been forgiving. But' – her voice grew soft – 'I wish it had turned out differently for Richard. We got Sasha back. But poor Jasmine. She lost her son for years.'

'I just had this wave of emotion at how young he looked,' Karl said. 'He just looks like a kid.'

'I hope they can make it,' Debbie said. 'I hope they don't get crushed.'

'He,' Karl corrected.

'Yeah,' Debbie said. 'I hope he doesn't get crushed.'

As Richard was being sentenced, Sasha was moving out of the dorms and into Epsilon Theta, which was housed in a yellow mansion about two miles from the MIT campus. A former Navy fraternity, it was now, as Sasha explained, 'a fraternity in name only.'

'I mean, we're dry, we're coed, we're a bunch of nerds,' they said. 'It's kind of like the anti-fraternity.' It was the perfect place for someone as shy as Sasha – a ready-made cadre of like-minded people. 'Whenever I'm not in class, I'm at ET,' Sasha explained.

The house had many eccentricities, one of which was that none of the bedrooms contained beds. The rooms were for studying or socialising only. All twenty-one Thetans slept in an attic dormitory that was kept perpetually dim and hushed so that house members could sleep undisturbed at any time of day.

When not sleeping or studying, Thetans were fond of video games, constructing and solving elaborate puzzles, playing, inventing, and reimagining board games, and pretending to kill one another as part of live-action Mafia games. They ate communal meals prepared by a cook named Karen, and had a variety of wry, nerdy traditions, like Not Coffee (defined as 'a weekly study break with tasty snacks that, in general, are not coffee') and Stereo Wars ('a contest of loudness before the start of Finals').

Sasha was the only nonbinary person in the house, but in response to their request, the house changed the names of the gendered bathrooms – known as 'heads' in a linguistic carryover from ET's Navy days – to 'men's plus' and 'women's plus.'

'Anyone who doesn't exclusively identify as male can use the women's head and anyone who doesn't exclusively identify as female can use the men's head,' Sasha explained. By this definition, Sasha could use both.

When Sasha came home for vacation, they proudly wore an Epsilon Theta sweatshirt. It was a little hard to tell that it was an ET sweatshirt, though, since both the letters and the sweatshirt were the exact same shade of purple.

They were happy at MIT. They'd found their people and they liked their classes. As for the fire, it was already a distant memory. Few people at MIT even knew it had happened.

Cherie sits in a café in Oakland, drinking a smoothie and talking about the old days, back when she and Richard were fourteen. She's wearing a turquoise tie-dyed T-shirt, jeans and gold hoop earrings. Her hair is waist-long and gleaming, her jewellery glittery, her skin flawless – except for the streaks made by the tears streaming down her face.

'It was kind of fucked up that we were out there fighting and cutting school,' she says. 'Let me just say that it was karma, you know? We should've been doing what we were supposed to be doing. Because look how it ended up for us.'

She ticked the outcomes off on her fingers. Skeet was dead. Ashley was a mum. Hadari and Jesse were serving time in the state penitentiary. Richard had been convicted of a felony.

She and Dae were the last ones standing. They were both

eighteen, but so far neither of them had graduated from high school. They weren't giving up on those diplomas, but they had a lot of catching up to do.

'It's just a sad story,' she says. 'When you think about it, it's just hella sad.'

MAIL DELIVERY

In January 2015, Sasha finally received the two letters Richard had written fourteen months earlier.

'I sympathised with him a lot, reading his letters,' Sasha said. 'It was definitely really moving, seeing his perspective.'

Debbie and Karl read the letters too.

'I'm kind of bummed that I didn't see them a year ago,' Karl said.

'It would've made a difference,' Debbie said. 'I would have been more engaged in what was going on with Richard, I think. For him to say, "I did wrong and I'm sorry and I hope you get better." That meant a lot to me.'

She sighed. 'If I'd read the letters, I would have had a different speech to give to him.'

On 2 January 2015, Richard left Alameda County Juvenile Hall in the back of a police car and travelled an hour and twenty minutes to Stockton, California. From there, the car motored down a long, straight road with plowed furrows and rows of trees on the left, brown grass on the right. Through a gate topped by razor wire, into a complex of low-slung white buildings with pitched blue roofs. This was N. A. Chaderjian Youth Correctional Facility, known as Chad, home to some two hundred and thirty males aged eighteen to twenty-five.

OPPORTUNITY

From the **Youth Rights Handbook** *distributed by the Division of Juvenile Justice:*

> After considering all the options, a decision was made by a Juvenile or Adult Court to commit or house you with the Division of Juvenile Justice (DJJ). Now that you are here, you may experience a feeling of anxiety or fear. This handbook was created to help you understand your rights, what to expect while housed in a facility of DJJ, answer some commonly asked questions, and provide useful information to help you while at DJJ.
>
> DJJ would like to see you successfully complete your stay and end your involvement with the criminal justice system. A number of our youth do

well here, and never find themselves in trouble again. When this happens, everyone benefits, and most importantly you. Think of your time here as an opportunity rather than a punishment and take advantage of all there is to offer. If you do this, there is no doubt that you will succeed and be better prepared when you are released into the community.

Basic Necessities

You have the right ...

To be provided with the basic things you need to live and stay healthy. Basic necessities include the right to:

- Healthy food
- Sleep
- Exercise
- A daily shower
- Medical services
- Reading material
- Contact with your parents, guardians, and attorney

- Clean water
- Bedding
- A drinking fountain
- A toilet
- Access to religious services
- Send and receive mail

Once you arrive at a Reception Center or Facility, you will be provided clean basic state-issued clothing and sufficient personal hygiene items. You will shower daily and are provided with soap, shampoo, towels, toothbrush, tooth paste, and other hygiene supplies. You may also choose to purchase other clothing and hygiene items through canteen.

SOME ITEMS AVAILABLE AT CANTEEN MAY INCLUDE:

- Clothing (pants, sweatshirts, thermals, name brand shoes)
- Food (snacks and soft drinks)
- Hygiene (lotion, hair products, makeup for female youth)
- Electronics (MP3 player and walkman)

Contraband

There are a number of items that are prohibited. Here are just a few:

- Cigarettes/tobacco
- Controlled substances
- Drug paraphernalia
- Drugs
- Gambling or lottery materials
- Gang writing or materials
- Money
- Sexually explicit drawings, pictures, prints, etc.
- Weapons or explosives
- Cell phones, PDA's, pagers, etc.

Searches

You have the right …

TO BE SEARCHED IN A WAY THAT IS LEAST EMBARRASSING TO YOU.

Searches are necessary to provide safety for you and others in your facility. There are different types of searches.

PROPERTY OR ROOM SEARCHES

Staff may search your room or possessions for contraband or evidence. Property and room searches should be conducted in your presence whenever possible. Staff will look through your clothing, bedding, books and all other belongings that are in your room.

PAT DOWN SEARCH

Clothed "pat-down" searches are conducted on a routine basis and are done in certain instances, like when a youth is leaving a vocational shop.

SKIN SEARCHES

Skin searches require you to remove your clothing. This will be conducted with maximum concern for your privacy and only peace officer or licensed medical staff of the same sex as you shall be present or participate in the search. Should you be suspected of concealing contraband in your rectal or vaginal area, a rectal or vaginal search may be conducted. This type of search will be performed by a licensed medical staff.

Ten years ago, California had 10,000 incarcerated juveniles in eleven state facilities and six camps. Today, the number hovers around 700, distributed among three facilities and one conservation camp, where low-risk youths do fire-suppression work. Only hard-core offenders come to Division of Juvenile Justice facilities – kids convicted of violent crimes and sex offences. (Youths convicted of less-serious crimes serve their time in county juvenile halls or group homes, or by remaining in the community while wearing GPS ankle monitors that track their movements.) Most of the young people in DJJ facilities were tried in juvenile court, as those who go through adult court usually wind up in adult prisons. Offenders who come here generally stay two or three years.

Chad has twelve living units, only nine of which are currently being used. They are arranged in a semicircle around a scrubby grass expanse where the youths play softball, touch football, soccer. It's blisteringly hot in the summer, bleakly cold in winter. The views are dreary: a bare brown hill, a chain-link fence, searchlights stacked on a pole. Yet despite the horrid weather, the squat sameness of the buildings, and the severity of the youths' offences, Chad doesn't feel like a terrible place. The atmosphere is relaxed and informal, more like a school than a prison. Youths go to class, attend vocational programmes, work at on-site jobs, take part in cognitive-behavioural counselling groups. They complain about being tired from work and from school, but they don't complain about being bored.

Ten years ago, Chad was a very different place. In August 2005, an eighteen-year-old named Joseph Daniel Maldonado hung himself with a bedsheet from the upper bunk of his room at Chad's Pajaro Hall. He had spent the previous eight weeks confined to his room close to twenty-four hours a day and had been denied mental health services despite his repeated requests. It was the fifth suicide at a California juvenile facility in as many years.

Back then, California's juvenile facilities were notoriously harsh, violent, dilapidated, dull and overcrowded, with young wards routinely subjected to solitary confinement, and some forced to exercise and attend classes while locked in cages. Use of physical force and psychotropic drugs was rampant. Violence hung about the place like a bad smell. Classes were frequently cancelled due to a shortage of teachers. Jobs were hard to come by, and vocational programmes were minimal. Correctional officers had the power to punish young inmates by adding time to their sentences, with the result that California juveniles were locked up almost three times longer than the national average. Even once they were released, California youths seemed unable to escape from the prisons' grasp. More than 80 per cent returned to state custody within three years of getting out.

A 2003 lawsuit, *Farrell vs. Harper*, led to wholesale reform. 'This is not a system that needs tinkering around the edges, this is a system that is broken almost everywhere you look,' a panel of state-approved correctional experts concluded in 2006. Later that year, the panel issued a plan for the complete restructuring of California's juvenile facilities.

It took time – and continual pressure from reformers – to implement the plan. But in fewer than ten years, California's juvenile facilities went from being some of the worst in the US to some of the best. 'They don't throw people in the hole very much, the violence is way down, the satisfaction of the staff and the kids is way up,' says Don Specter, executive director of the not-for-profit Prison Law Office, which filed the original lawsuit in 2002 and has been tracking the state's progress ever since. 'It's a totally different place.'

Instead of focusing exclusively on punishing bad behaviour, staff now track and reward good behaviour. Youths get 'positive checks' for complying with the rules, but also for using the interpersonal skills necessary to do well on the outside – skills like asking for help or talking through a conflict. Behave well all day and you can stay an hour later in the common areas instead of having to return to your room at eight p.m. Do well all week and you snag candy, chips, or soda from the 'incentive locker.' A month of good behaviour wins you an invitation to a pizza or nacho party. And if you do well for long enough, you can apply for a weeklong stay in one of two 'incentive rooms,' cells that have been converted into mini–man caves, with DirecTV, video game consoles, comfy bedding, and – of crucial importance in stiflingly hot Stockton – a fan.

'**Let me ask you,**' **Ricky Lindsey said.** 'Do you have risky thoughts going on throughout your day?'

Lindsey, a parole agent at Chad, was addressing Richard and a half dozen other young men in a small meeting room inside Chad's Feather Hall, the living quarters for the facility's lowest-risk, best-behaving youths. It was late afternoon. The young inmates had completed school and work for the day. Now they had just one more obligation before dinner – CounterPoint, a cognitive-behavioural programme designed to teach problem-solving and perspective-taking.

'Fear of getting in trouble,' offered a young man in a white T-shirt. He tipped his chair back against the whiteboard behind him. The room, bare except for an easel, wasn't much larger than a walk-in cupboard. Richard sat quietly, elbows on his knees, listening.

'What would get you in trouble, though?' Lindsey asked. He was a genial fireplug of a man who spoke informally, like someone from the neighbourhood.

'Like, behaviour.'

'What kind of behaviour gets you in trouble?'

'Anger.'

'What makes you angry?'

'Rage.'

'What makes you rageful? Come on.'

'Disrespect.'

'When you feel disrespected, how does that make you feel?'

'It hurts.'

'It hurts? What does it make you want to think?'

'My feelings be like wanting me to react,' the young man said.

'Justification?' another youth offered. He had short hair, and his confident manner signaled that he'd been around awhile.

'Why would that go to risky thinking?'

'Most people don't think before they act,' the youth with glasses explained. 'I think, but with that thinking I still try to justify what I'm going to do. I'm a little stubborn with my thinking.'

Lindsey nodded as if to say, *Now we're getting there.*

'Risky thinking,' he said. 'All of you are here for a reason, right? I'm going to say that all of you are here because of some risky thoughts you had. Maybe I shouldn't have went to the store that night. Maybe I shouldn't have jacked that guy that night. Maybe I shouldn't have had a fight with that guy that night. Right? Maybe I shouldn't have had that pistol on me that night. Right? Just sayin'.'

'Or is it because you *didn't* think about it?' another kid suggested. He wore a black jacket and had a sardonic edge to him.

'It could be,' Lindsey agreed. 'Other guys be under the influence. Not being fully aware of your surroundings can be risky thinking because you're not in your right state of mind. How do you know it's a risky thought?'

'Doubt,' said a youth whose hair was pulled back in a ponytail. He leaned forward and rested his elbows on his knees, his eyes on Lindsey.

'Doubt,' Lindsey repeated. 'Explain.'

'When your conscience tells you it's bad, you know you ain't supposed to do it.'

'Your conscience,' Lindsey said. 'That little angel and that little devil.'

'And you listen to the bad one,' the ponytailed kid said. 'The good one is the one you're *supposed* to listen to. The good one is the one that's basically – that's *you*.'

'The good one is giving you that gut feeling,' offered the kid with the black-framed glasses.

'He's saying, "You sure that's the right thing to do?"' Lindsey agreed. 'So you got a good dude and a bad dude, which one are you going to listen to?'

'I think I got two bad dudes,' said the boy in the black jacket. He grinned.

Lindsey laughed. 'It's different for everybody.' He handed out a sheet of paper listing different kinds of risky thinking. '"Overgeneralising." What's that?'

'"You always blame it on me,"' the kid with the glasses said, playing the role of the overgeneraliser. ' "Staff's always trying to get me. You always give me negative checks." '

Lindsey nodded. 'There you go.' He ran through some other categories. 'Catastrophising' – that was one kid's grandma, always sure the worst was going to happen. 'Desperate and Deserving'?

'You're like, "I need this," or "I have a right to this," ' somebody offered.

'Uh-oh,' Lindsey said.

'Sort of entitlement,' someone else suggested. ' "Man, why can't I ever have this?" '

'Ah.' Lindsey raised his eyebrows, asking for more.

' "Ain't I a good person? Don't I deserve to have this? Man, I've been working this job for five years. I still don't have this?" '

A discussion ensued. Was 'Desperate and Deserving' just a way that poor people thought?

'Rich people can't be "Desperate and Deserving" – what are you talking about?' one kid scoffed.

'They can be hella rich and they can be like, "I deserve to have a wife" and you start to feel hella bad for yourself,' the ponytailed kid said. 'Like some people got so much money, but they don't have nobody.'

'Yeah, but I'd rather be them than be here,' the sardonic kid said. He folded his arms across his chest.

Everybody nodded.

PROGRESS REPORT

Sasha stood in the hallway outside Department 11, wearing a vest, button-up shirt, and bow tie paired with a long skirt and ballet flats. Over their shoulder they had slung a canvas bag decorated with pins. *LGBTQ class of 2018*, read one. Another said simply: *they/them/their.* They'd cut their hair short and shaved it on one side. The ends were dyed fluorescent pink.

Debbie and Karl stood beside Sasha. They too were dressed in their courtroom best: a purple jersey dress for Debbie; pleated trousers, a pink checked shirt and a tie for Karl. Karl had topped his outfit with his hat, the same one he'd used to cover Sasha the day Sasha was burned.

It was the last Friday in June 2015. The family had come to court for Richard's second progress report – the one that would determine whether he was eligible for resentencing. Richard had passed the first hurdle with flying colours. He'd had no disciplinary violations and the staff at Chad had described him as motivated to participate in treatment programmes and remorseful about his crime. If his second progress report was equally positive, he could be resentenced to five years instead of seven.

The lift opened and Jasmine stepped out, wearing jeans and high-tops and a black-and-white shawl-collared jacket. She hugged all three members of Sasha's family and took a seat, exhaling sharply. The strain was gone from her face and she was smiling, but she was tired too, having recently taken on a second job. After completing her shift at the convalescent home, she now worked a four-hour shift at the supermarket, often not getting off work until one a.m. Every Sunday, she drove a three-hour round-trip to visit Richard.

Getting the time off to come to court hadn't been easy. Her boss had turned down her request, but she had managed to quietly trade shifts with a co-worker. Now there was another problem. Richard's court file had somehow been misplaced, which meant that the judge couldn't review the record. The case would have to be continued until the following week. Jasmine's shoulders slumped. 'I can't get more time off,' she whispered.

She kept talking for a moment, but then her voice trailed off. 'I'm smiling, but I'm crying inside,' she admitted. She was cycling through the options in her mind – how could she get there? Who else could come?

The case file mishap wasn't just a problem for Jasmine. Sasha's family wanted to address the court, but they were leaving for vacation the next day. They wouldn't be around next week.

After some discussion, Judge Delucchi agreed to let them make their statement. He beckoned Karl to the front of the room.

The parties now stood before the judge like a couple standing before the altar – Karl with deputy district attorney Scott Ford at his side, Richard with Bill Du Bois. In the year and a half since it all began, Richard had grown taller than Du Bois, his shoulders broader. He watched Karl, his expression neutral.

Karl cleared his throat and unfolded a sheet of paper.

'I am speaking on behalf of my wife, Debbie ——, and our child, Sasha ——. Thank you for the opportunity to have our voices heard,' he began. The courtroom fell silent.

'In the week following the fire on the bus, Richard —— wrote two letters to Sasha, in which he took full responsibility for his actions, and asked for forgiveness. Unfortunately, it took fourteen months for those letters to reach us. When we finally read them, we were moved to tears. The letters gave us a clearer picture of who Richard is, and we wished we had been able to see them before Debbie spoke at the sentencing hearing.'

As he listened, Richard's jaw worked, the muscles tensing and relaxing. His lips pulled to one side.

'I *believe* Richard when he says he meant no bodily harm to Sasha,' Karl continued. 'But I also believe that Sasha would not have been a target if Sasha had been wearing jeans.' He described how other kids on the bus had laughed even as Sasha's clothes went up in flames. 'We wish for Richard and those other kids to learn empathy towards those who are different. We hope that there are programmes in juvenile detention that can at least help Richard with this, and that he can become an ally who will stand up against the bullying and hatred of gay and trans people.'

It was so quiet in the courtroom that you could hear the flutter of Karl's breath as he tried to steady his voice.

'From the start we have been opposed to Richard's being tried as an adult,' he said. 'His actions appear to have been impulsive, immature and unpremeditated. He did make a big mistake and recognises that. He asked for our forgiveness.' Karl's voice broke. 'Sasha, Debbie and I *have* forgiven Richard,' he whispered. 'We hope the state will focus more on preparing him for the world beyond incarceration than on punishing him.'

When Karl raised his eyes from the paper clenched in his hands, he saw Richard watching him.

Thank you, Richard mouthed.

At the back of the courtroom, the Ladies were red-eyed and sniffling.

'Given that the sentence allows the court a pretty fair amount of discretion, I do not take your words lightly,' Judge Delucchi said. Then he continued the case to the following Tuesday.

'The record should reflect that the court has read the fairly voluminous records that have been provided,' Judge Delucchi said when Richard returned to court the next week.

It was a positive report, the judge noted. Richard was attending school, participating in treatment, and had expressed interest in getting a job at the facility. He hadn't had any disciplinary actions. The staff noted that he was reserved and quiet and tended to keep to himself, but they commended him for limiting his interactions 'so that he is not drawn into too much negativity.'

All in all, Delucchi told Richard, the report indicated 'a level of maturity that you didn't exhibit on the day of the offence.' In addition, he continued, '[Sasha's] family has made it clear what their position is, and that should be considered.'

With that, he modified Richard's sentence from seven years to five years. With credit for time served, he would be out just before his twenty-first birthday. It was his recommendation that Richard serve the totality of that time in the juvenile system.

Jasmine's boss had given her the day off to attend the hearing. When it was over, she stood smiling in the hallway, looking slightly dazed.

'It's still a long time,' she said. 'Three years.'

She had spent the weekend with her cousin Regis, attending the San Francisco LGBT Pride celebration. Now she was planning to take advantage of the rare day off and do some errands. First on the list: wash her car.

'It's such a release,' she said in the lift. She leaned her head back against the wall and raised her eyes to the ceiling before correcting herself. 'Relief.'

Five months after Richard was sentenced, Andrew and Sasha got together for dinner at a Latin American café in Berkeley. They hadn't seen each other much over the previous couple of years, but now Sasha was in town for winter break and they were getting together for the second time in as many weeks. They'd already had that initial 'What are you up to these days?' conversation, and over dinner they just talked, the way they used to, about the world and what it was and what it should be. They talked about revolution vs. reform and anarchism vs. socialism, and Andrew was struck, as he always had been, by the way Sasha carefully considered things instead of just echoing the opinions of other people.

Andrew was eighteen now. His glasses were rimless at the bottom; his nose pierced at the septum. He identified as a gay man. Few people knew his trans status – he kept it on the down low.

Yet when straight men treated him like a bro, he felt a familiar sense of disorientation. 'For how vehemently I felt like I wasn't a girl, I have to say, being a boy isn't super great either,' he admitted. 'Both sides have such bullshit baggage attached to them.'

If being a man meant always having to act confident and never being able to admit feeling sadness or self-doubt, it was just as much of a trap as being a woman was. He was happier now than he'd been before he transitioned, but he still yearned for something else, some place outside of gender.

'Actually,' he said, 'I'm starting to identify a little bit as – I don't even know the word I want to use yet. I like *androgynous*. I like *genderqueer*.'

What held him back? Fear. Fear of other people's judgements, their questions, their hostility, their fascination.

'Because I fall neatly within the binary, I feel comfortable right now,' he explained. 'But if I were to radically shift my appearance in a way that was more androgynous, I don't know how comfortable that would be for me. I mean, I've already been asked enough questions about my genitals. I'm just done with that.'

BIRTHDAYS

Richard turned eighteen in Alameda County Juvenile Hall, just before being transferred back to Chad. Individual birthdays aren't celebrated in Juvenile Hall, so it was a day exactly like any other day. Richard was used to that by now. He hadn't spent a birthday at home since he'd turned fourteen. His fifteenth, sixteenth, seventeenth, and now eighteenth birthdays had all been spent locked up.

Back at Chad, Richard earned his high school diploma and then began taking vocational classes, earning certificates in programmes like Irrigation Design and Forklift Driving. He worked in the barbershop for a while, then got a job working for Free Venture, an environmentally certified not-for-profit that refurbishes and recycles e-waste on-site. At Free Venture he earned $9.70 an hour, which allowed him to start paying off the $2,100 he'd been fined as part of his plea bargain, and also deposit money into a savings account for his eventual release. It was one of the best jobs at the facility, and one of the hardest to get, but Richard was doing exceptionally well. He had already attained Incentive Level A, the highest incentive level a young inmate could achieve, and he was housed among other low-risk youths in a hall where the atmosphere was generally relaxed. In the evenings kids watched TV or played Ping-Pong and dominoes in the dayroom, or settled in to make phone calls at one of the two pay phones.

Richard held himself a bit aloof – slow to trust, slow to warm. He didn't smile much. Each night, he returned to a six-by-eight-foot cell with a metal sink and toilet. On his desk, he kept a Bible, some folded paper crafts and a television he had purchased with money he'd earned at Free Venture. Neat rows of family snapshots were taped to the wall. All the people he loved the most, bright-eyed, grinning, frozen in time.

He slept in the lower berth of a metal bunk bed. The top berth had no mattress and he used it to display the vocational and educational certificates he'd earned at Chad, the squares of coloured paper arranged in orderly lines.

Beside them, he placed a printout of the poem 'Invictus' by William Ernest Henley:

> *Out of the night that covers me,*
> *Black as the pit from pole to pole,*
> *I thank whatever gods may be*
> *For my unconquerable soul.*

In the fell clutch of circumstance
I have not winced nor cried aloud.
Under the bludgeonings of chance
My head is bloody, but unbowed.

He had another two birthdays still to celebrate behind bars, his nineteenth and his twentieth. Sometime before his twenty-first, a police car would take him back to Alameda County Juvenile Hall, where he would be processed and then released.

After that, he would finally complete the journey home he began on the afternoon of 4 November 2013.

After that, the next chapter of his life would finally begin.

In January 2016, just before going back to school for their second year of college, Sasha and Michael got together at Maybeck to play the index card game. The game was still fun, the in-jokes still funny, even if some of the references had been lost in the mists of time. Sasha could still effortlessly layer a lisp over a Russian accent when the cards required it. Michael still wore a gray beanie, which was good because there was still a card that said *Steal Michael's beanie.*

'Have you ever heard of a little word called *they*?' Sasha remarked after pulling Lunesta Sleeping Pills, a card that used *he/she* pronouns (*Player must play with his/her forehead on the table*).

It was an old line, one that dated from when Sasha was first trying to get people to remember gender-neutral pronouns.

Except now it was a joke instead of a reminder. Nobody needed reminding except the card, which had been written before Sasha was Sasha.

A couple of days earlier, Michael and Sasha had digitally scanned the full stack of index cards for posterity. As they went through the deck, they'd paused over the ones that mentioned someone named Luke.

One featured a drawing of a pen and a bottle of ink. Luke's Fountain Pen, it said. *Draw a card.*

It was kind of a weak pun – not nearly as good as many of the cards that came later. But after talking it over, the two decided to leave the Luke cards in the deck.

After all, Sasha said, they were part of the historical record.

A lot had changed since the beginning of high school, including Sasha's name, pronouns and style of dress. But in all the important ways, Sasha was still Sasha. They still loved cats, cartoons, games and hats. And they were still, as they'd once written on their blog, *the biggest bus nerd u will ever meet.*

Now that love of buses had become an academic focus. They had decided to major in urban planning and hoped to eventually get a job designing or improving public transport systems. 'I might *take* public transit even if I wasn't in love with it,' Sasha explained. 'But the reason I'm *studying* it is because I have this personal love for it.'

That love, well, you could ask Sasha to explain it, but you'd be wasting your time. They could no more explain loving buses than they could explain loving the colour purple. 'I'm an autistic kid with a special interest,' Sasha said, and smiled. 'That's probably the best answer I can give.'

SOME GENDER-NEUTRALITY MILESTONES

2007

Nepal's Supreme Court orders the government to issue citizenship ID cards that allow people to describe themselves as 'third-gender' or 'other.'

2013

Australia gives citizens a choice of three official genders: male, female and X.

Germany gives parents a choice of three gender options when filling out a newborn's birth certificate: male, female and indeterminate.

2014

Facebook begins allowing users to self-identify as something other than male or female.

Denmark gives its citizens the choice of three official genders: male, female and X.

2015

The White House designates a gender-neutral bathroom for visitors and staff.

Target announces they're removing gender-based signs from their toy and furnishings aisles.

Malta and Nepal join the list of countries offering their citizens the choice of an official third gender.

The *Oxford English Dictionary* adds the gender-neutral prefix *Mx* to its lexicon as an alternative to *Mr*, *Ms*, *Mrs* and *Miss*. It also adds the word *cisgender*.

Disney removes the gender categories from its Halloween costumes.

The *Washington Post* updates its style manual to allow writers to use the pronoun *they* to refer to an individual, calling it 'the only sensible solution to English's lack of a gender-neutral third-person singular personal pronoun.'

The American Dialect Society chooses the singular gender-neutral pronoun *they* as their Word of the Year.

Amiko-Gabriel Blue, a resident of Ashland, Oregon, goes to court to legally change their gender to 'neutral'. The request is denied but afterward the judge tells a reporter, 'I would have been happy to do it if I thought it was legal.'

2016

North Carolina passes the Public Facilities Privacy and Security Act, requiring people to use public bathrooms according to the biological sex on their birth certificate.

Merriam-Webster adds the words *cisgender* and *genderqueer* to the dictionary.

The Obama administration directs the nation's schools to provide students with access to bathrooms and locker rooms that match their chosen gender identity.

A retired US Army sergeant named Jamie Shupe receives permission from an Oregon court to legally change their gender to nonbinary, becoming the first US person to do so.

2017

After losing, according to Politifact, an estimated $500 million dollars in revenue and the chance to host the 2017 NBA All-Star game, North Carolina lawmakers vote to repeal the state's Public Facilities Privacy and Security Act, known as 'the bathroom bill'. But while the replacement legislation eliminates the requirement that people use the bathroom for the gender they were assigned at birth, it keeps state legislators in charge of future bathroom policies.

The Trump administration eliminates the Obama administration guidelines that directed schools to provide transgender students with access to bathrooms and locker rooms matching their gender identity.

The Showtime drama *Billions* introduces Taylor, television's first nonbinary character.

The MTV Movie and TV Awards become the first major acting awards to eliminate gendered categories for performance. Emma Watson won the all-inclusive category Best Actor award, which was presented by nonbinary actor Asia Kate Dillon.

SOME NUMBERS: US JUVENILE INCARCERATION

(Figures are the most current available as of 2016)

Number of juveniles held in correctional facilities on any given day: 54,148.

Average cost of juvenile incarceration for one twelve-month stay: $146,302.

Percentage of juveniles who are African American: 16.

Percentage of incarcerated youths who are African American: 41.

Percentage of African American youths who do their time in an adult prison: 58.

Number of people currently serving life sentences without the possibility of parole for crimes committed as juveniles: 2,570.

Cost of incarcerating one juvenile for life: $2.5 million.

Percentage increase in the likelihood that a person will be incarcerated as an adult if they have been incarcerated as a juvenile: between 22 and 41.

Percentage of confined youths who have witnessed someone severely injured or killed: 70.

Percentage of confined youths who report having been physically or sexually abused in their lifetime: 30.

Percentage of confined youths who have been sexually assaulted while in custody: 9.5.

Percentage of confined youths who have attempted suicide: 22.

ACKNOWLEDGMENTS

So many people have been so generous with their time, expertise, recollections and insights as I was researching this book that it would take another book just to thank them properly. Here are a few of them.

Sujatha Baliga, nuri nusrat, Kate McCracken, Anna Blackshaw, Maria Dominguez, and Darris Young shared their knowledge and insights about the legal proceedings. Bill Du Bois patiently fielded my incessant inquiries, as did Teresa Drenick and Nancy O'Malley. Assistant superintendent Brian Hopson at Alameda County Probation Department and assistant superintendent Craig Watson at N. A. Chaderjian Youth Correctional Facility were gracious guides through their respective institutions.

Staff at both Oakland High School and Maybeck High School took time to talk with me despite having their own demanding jobs to do. A heartfelt thanks to Matin Abdel-Qawi, Arianna Caplan, Carlitta Collins, Earnest Jenkins III, Tiago Robinson, Jesse

Shapiro, Orlando Watkins, Amy Wilder and especially Kaprice Wilson at Oakland High School. Grateful thanks also to William Webb and Trevor Cralle at Maybeck.

This book started out as an article for *The New York Times Magazine*, where Dean Robinson, Jessica Lustig, Bill Wasik and Jake Silverstein improved it in countless ways. Both at the *Times Magazine* and later through his own outfit, the Verificationist, Rob Liguori pinned down facts and contributed observations of his own. Without him, there would be no sandwich. Any remaining errors are my own.

Filmmaker Lonny Shavelson generously gave me access to interviews and raw footage from his wonderful documentary about nonbinary people, *Three to Infinity*. Important parts of this book were seen through his eyes.

The description of the Oakland High basketball team's pregame huddle is taken from *Playing for Sasha, Playing Against Hate*, a short film by the Oakland nonprofit Not in Our Town. I discovered the still-timely quote from John P. Altgeld in the fascinating book *Juvenile Justice in the Making* by David S. Tanenhaus. Many young people took time to talk with me. Some were quoted, some were not, and some asked not to be named, but all helped make this book what it is. Thank you to Michael Birkhead, Carrie Carpenter, Teah Cory, Ian Gonzer, Eve Irwin, Thomas Kelly, Cherie, Healy Miller, Emarieay Prescott, Willie Scott III, Sabrina Tern, as well as Andrew, Nemo, Liam, Lidell, TC, Jeff, J. and Pancha.

Every writer should be lucky enough to have an agent like Erin Murphy and an editor like Joy Peskin – smart, savvy, committed and kind. They have been guiding beacons throughout.

I'm grateful to both Alex Gino and Nicholas Henderson for reading and commenting with tremendous sensitivity and thoughtfulness. Thanks also to Nancy Elgin and Chandra Wohleber for going over the text with a fine-tooth comb.

My husband and son were always there to talk things over with me during the three years I spent researching, writing and ruminating. Their love, wisdom and humour made everything easier, and their expertise on many matters was indispensable.

No words are adequate to describe my debt to the two families whose stories are at the heart of this book. Their grace, kindness and compassion were an inspiration to me throughout. Sorry you had to put up with me for so long.

CREDITS

Excerpt from "Hir" included with the permission of Alysia Nicole Harris and Aysha El Shamayleh.

Excerpt from the Division of Juvenile Justice 2010 *Youth Rights Handbook* included with the permission of the California Department of Corrections and Rehabilitation.